RESCUE FROM PLOESTI

The Harry Fritz Story — A World War II Triumph

By

William G. Williams

WHITE MANE BOOKS
SHIPPENSBURG, PENNSYLVANIA

This White Mane Books publication
was printed by
Beidel Printing House, Inc.
63 West Burd Street
Shippensburg, PA 17257-0708 USA

The acid-free paper used in this book meets the guidelines for permanence and durability of the Committee on Production Guidelines for Book Longevity of the Council on Library Resources.

For a complete list of available publications
please write
White Mane Books
Division of White Mane Publishing Company, Inc.
P.O. Box 708
Shippensburg, PA 17257-0708 USA

Library of Congress Cataloging-in-Publication Data

Williams, William G.
    Rescue from Ploesti : the Harry Fritz story : a World War II triumph / by William G. Williams.
        p. cm.
    Includes bibliographical references (p.) and index.
    ISBN 1-57249-340-2 (acid-free paper)
    1. Fritz, Harry B. 2. World War, 1939-1945--Prisoners and prisons, Romanian. 3.
Prisoners of war--United States--Biography. 4. Ploieðti, Battles of, Ploieðti, Romania,
1943-1944. 5. United States. Army Air Forces--Biography. 6. World War,
1939-1945--Aerial operations, American. 7. B-24 bomber. I. Title.

D805.R66W55 2003
940.54'72498'092--dc21
[B]

                                                                            2003052512

PRINTED IN THE UNITED STATES OF AMERICA

*Dedicated to all American airmen of World War II
who did not come home.*

CONTENTS

WORDS FROM VETERANS

"The 15th Air Force was activated on 1 November, 1943. It ceased operations on 10 May, 1945. During that time it had 3,544 B-24 Liberators and 1,407 B-17 Fortresses assigned. In those eighteen months, 1,756 Liberators and 624 Fortresses were lost in combat—a loss rate of 48 percent. Why so many losses? In Europe in those days the three toughest targets were Berlin, Vienna and Ploesti. The 15th had two of the three in its area of operations.

"Attacking Ploesti was as close to visiting Hell as one could imagine. I know because I went there three times—5 April, 24 April and 5 May, 1944.

"Imagine a bomb run of twenty miles straight and level on a fixed course approaching a large dark cloud of bursting flak shells into which groups in front would literally disappear into the smoke. When you got there the flak bursts were not only all around you but above and below. And then, outside the flak area were the fighters waiting to pounce on the cripples. How did we make it through that holocaust and so many others didn't? I have no answer except that God needed us for other things.

"Sergeant Fritz had a lot of company in his prison camp. My own Group, the 449th, contributed over ninety POWs shot down over Ploesti. And you could figure that the guys who bailed out represented about 40 percent of the casualties sustained."

—Donald R. Currier, Lieutenant Colonel, USAF (Ret)

(Lieutenant Colonel Currier retired from the U.S. Air Force in 1969 after twenty-six years of active duty. He was twenty-two years old when he flew his first combat mission as a B-24 navigator from a 15th Air Force base in southern Italy. He completed his full tour of duty there as a first lieutenant. He now lives in Smithburg, Maryland, and is the author of *50 Mission Crush*, the story of his own World War II experiences.)

* * * * *

"*Rescue from Ploesti: The Harry Fritz Story — A World War II Triumph*, by author William G. Williams, is dedicated to all American airmen of World War II who did not come home. In his choice of subject, and in his motivation, author Williams is earning the thanks of every airman who wore the uniform and who was one of the 'lucky' ones who returned safely home. The author is also honoring a lesser known member of the aircrew who was nevertheless part of the discipline and teamwork required for the mission.

"As the pilot and aircraft commander of a heavy bomber (B-17), I have been concerned that World War II is becoming just a footnote in history, and that those who served in a battle that set a new course for the world would soon become an asterisk. Thanks to the efforts of authors like Mr. Williams, we can learn of the dedication of individuals like Harry Fritz, who were part of a unit trained to work together.

"Aircrews were teams, and within themselves were proud and responsible to themselves, to each other, and to their country. As a training procedure, I required each member of my crew to ride the seat and carry out the assignment of other members of the crew. That included myself, and I must admit that my 'pilot's swagger' was not as pronounced after I had flown half an hour in the ball turret or the tail gunner's perch. We may have been young men in age (low twenties), but maturity came beyond our years as the mission assigned us became more evident.

"The tail gunner may have been the 'butt' of jokes because he never knew where we were going, but could only see where he had been. The ball turret gunner was like an unattached balloon who had to be an 'airhead' to even crawl into his nest. The navigator, of course, could go nowhere without a road map with railroad tracks on it. But of such was the camaraderie that built love, respect and discipline on an aircrew. And then, when the morning briefing said 'Ploesti', every man on the crew knew that he was important to the mission and to the safe return of his crew.

"Author Williams has done a remarkable job on his research of one of the decisive missions of the war, and his selection of Harry Fritz will endear his work to every aircrew. We are pleased that he has asked us to fly as his wingman on this flight."

—Will Ketner

(Mr. Ketner was a B-17 pilot with the 303rd Bomb Group, 8th Air Force, at Molesworth, England. He was twenty-one years old when he flew his first combat mission as a copilot and twenty-three when he returned to the United States as a first lieutenant. He says the number of missions each man flew was not the important factor, it was whether he got home safely. He recounts the story of a friend, George Klaus, who had only flown five missions, was shot down over Europe, lost both legs and was a POW for two years. Mr. Ketner now lives in Harrisburg, Pennsylvania.)

INTRODUCTION

Less than one month after his twenty-first birthday, Staff Sergeant Harry B. Fritz bailed out of his falling bomber into German captivity, thus becoming another victim in the long struggle to close the oil pipeline to Adolf Hitler's rampaging planes, ships, tanks and motorized equipment. In 1944, Fritz and thousands of other American army airmen were part of a vast armada of bomber crews and fighter pilots who, despite heavy losses, sought to stop the engines of German military might.

One of the targets frequently visited in the last twelve months of World War II in Europe was the city of Ploesti in southern Romania. The attraction was not Ploesti itself but eleven oil refineries which surrounded it or were located nearby — the source of a third of Germany's oil supplies. Romania had reluctantly become aligned with the Axis powers, led by Germany in the European Theater.

Without oil, World War II armies could not move. Oil powered the German navy's surface ships and submarines; it rushed the Wehrmacht's tanks, artillery batteries and supply trucks over the roads of Europe and Africa and into Russia; and it kept the Luftwaffe's fighters and bombers airborne.

Romania had the oil, mainly from the foothills of the Transylvanian Alps, and Ploesti had the plants to refine it into gasoline, lubricants and other byproducts for the huge industrial and military appetite. The complex surrounding the city at the mouth of the Prahova Valley had the rail lines, pipelines, roads and a tributary of the Danube River to transport it.

Romania, with a heavy dose of poverty, had relied primarily on foreign capital — including Germany, Great Britain and the United States — to build the oil complex before the First World War. Romania perhaps had little choice in its initial partner in 1939; its economy was tied strongly to Germany and its location made Britain, France and the United States quite distant. To cement that relationship, German troops marched into the country in September 1940, ostensibly on a request from Romania's pro-German prime minister, General Ion Antonescu, that Romania needed military protection for its industry. The relationship, however, was not universal and in January 1941 German tanks had to put down a citizen revolt on the streets of Bucharest.

Except for its 143-mile coast line on the Black Sea, Romania is landlocked. Its western border was shared with Hungary, also in the Axis camp, and with Yugoslavia, which sided with the Allies. To its south was Bulgaria, another Axis member. The Black Sea took a portion of the eastern border, but most of that border and all of the northern line were shared with Russia, an Allied power which struggled early in World War II against the powerful Nazi onslaught.

Ploesti, until 1944, was an extremely difficult target to reach. The Allies did not have long-range bombers that could fly to it easily nor did they have fighters with the necessary range to protect the bombers. When they captured southern Italy and opened airfields there they were still a long flight over the Adriatic Sea and Yugoslavian airspace from those inviting refinery targets.

"Oil was the Achilles heel of the German Wehrmacht (armed forces) and the big Ploesti refineries in Romania produced one-third of all this precious liquid Hitler needed to run his 'blitzkrieg.' It was No. 1 target on Allied planning boards," wrote U.S. Air Force Major James F. Sunderman.[1]

"The obliteration of this vital segment of national and military life, more than any other factor, brought on the quick collapse of the Third Reich by depriving it of its mobility," according to Sunderman. "Lack of oil strangled the economy and paralyzed the once powerful Wehrmacht. It eliminated Germany as an industrial nation."

In 1943, Allied leaders knew that to reach Ploesti they needed to neutralize Germany's powerful air force, establish bases closer than the African continent and develop fighters that could escort heavy bombers to and from a target. Therefore, the first order of business for the U.S. 15th Air Force in Africa, the U.S. 8th Air Force in Great Britain and Britain's Royal Air Force Bomber Command became the destruction of factories which produced Germany's fighter aircraft. But there was also a need for a daring raid to shake up the enemy and raise Allied morale—much like the surprise attack on Tokyo in April 1942 by a fleet of sixteen U.S. Army B-25 bombers led by Lieutenant Colonel James H. Doolittle from the deck of the aircraft carrier USS *Hornet*. (On November 1, 1943, Major General James H. Doolittle took command of the 15th Air Force in Italy.)

Such a raid was carried out on June 11, 1942, by twelve B-24 Liberators led by Colonel Harry A. Halverson. It was a long and difficult flight from a forward Allied base in Egypt across the Mediterranean and into the southern belly of Europe. All twelve planes eventually returned to base, but their bombing run over Ploesti did little damage and it alerted the Germans to the vulnerability of the refineries, at least to air attacks. It would be more than a year before the Army Air Force had the men and the machines to visit Ploesti again.

The Allied plan to cripple the Nazi fuel supply called for RAF Bomber Command to hit petroleum plants in Germany. The U.S. 8th Air Force in Great Britain would go after targets in parts of Germany, Czechoslovakia and Poland. The assignments for the 15th Air Force from Africa and then Italy were southern Germany, southern Poland, Austria, Hungary, Italy, southern France and the Balkan countries, including oil-rich Romania.

Bombing strategists saw great advantages in hitting oil refineries. To begin, refineries were easier to find than oil wells, which were squirreled away in hilly and wooded areas. Secondly, it took a lot of work for the Axis countries to retrieve oil from the ground, store it in tanks and ship it to the refineries, so bombing the refineries would mean a great deal of wasted effort at the well sites, storage areas and shipping lines.

In addition, for the most part refineries were large targets covering wide areas. They were mostly above ground. There was a great deal of material which would explode and burn. Smokestacks, some reaching one hundred feet, could be seen easily from a distance. And the facilities were pinpointed by immense metal holding tanks, by conglomerations of industrial buildings, and by networks of roads, pipelines and rail lines which brought in the crude oil and took out the finished products. They were well-marked targets.

In addition, the planners knew that to put a refinery out of operation for a period of time it was only necessary to knock out one function of the complex. When the cracking plant or the boiler house or any other component was damaged or destroyed, the flow of oil stopped until repairs could be made.

But there were also hazards for bomber crews. Oil refineries in the Ploesti area were well defended by German and Romanian fighters from eight airbases within seventy miles, by at least one hundred anti-aircraft guns, and by a like number of barrage balloons tethered to the ground with steel cables. The defenders had also installed some two thousand smoke pots which could blot out the entire target from a bombardier's sight. And they had built brick blast walls around every structure to prevent a direct hit on one from having a domino effect on the next. The walls went as as high as twenty feet. Some were as wide as six feet at the bottom and two feet at the top.

There were two rings of defenses at Ploesti, an inner ring from the refineries out to four miles, and an outer ring which extended out to twenty-two miles. In addition, the Germans had built two fake Ploestis, one six miles west and the other six miles east of the real town. The one to the east — designed to draw night attacks — had lights resembling a refinery. It even had an oil pool which could be fired to make airmen believe they had hit a target.

The Ploesti complex was immense: eleven refineries covering nineteen square miles connected by rail tracks. Nine of the refineries surrounded Ploesti itself; one was at Brazi, three miles to the south; and one was at Campina, eighteen miles northwest. One of the Ploesti refineries was so large that it covered a mile of ground. The potential output of the eleven sites was more than 700,000 tons of oil every month. Before the war, the refineries had been mainly financed by Germany, Great Britain and the United States.

In an early 1945 report to his group and wing commanders, Lieutenant General Ira C. Eaker, commander of the Mediterranean Allied Air Forces, wrote that "the enemy can protect some industries from strategic bombardment by dividing them into a great number of small units, which present difficult targets. Neither synthetic oil plants nor crude oil refineries can easily be dispersed in this manner."[2]

Eaker explained the reason for delay after the inconsequential June 1942 attack on Ploesti, saying: "...the systematic attack on oil did not commence until the late spring and summer of 1944. The Strategic Air Forces delayed their attack until they could do a thorough job." In other words, Eaker needed more planes, more men, more bombs, more fighter protection, and closer airfields to shut down Ploesti.

The general knew that moderate and temporary reductions in the oil supply line would not be fatal to the Nazi cause. He also knew that Allied attacks would have to be sustained over a period of months because the Germans had plenty of spare parts and slave laborers (military prisoners and conscripted civilians) who could fix damaged plants fairly quickly.

He reasoned that three conditions had to be met before his bomber crews could be successful:

"First, they required bases within range of the entire Axis oil industry, including the vital Ploesti region. Suitable bases were not acquired until 15th Air Force began operating from Foggia (southern Italy) at the end of 1943.

"Second, they required a sufficiently large striking force to attack 84 targets and to keep them under attack at regular intervals.

"Finally, they required air supremacy in order to enable the striking force to penetrate deep into enemy territory to attack remote targets in Central and Eastern Germany. This supremacy was achieved in the spring of 1944. By that time, our strategic bombardment of fighter aircraft factories had completely disrupted the enemy's plan for expanding his defensive fighter force. Equally important, we had long-range fighters capable of escorting our bombers all the way to the target."

Half of the Axis oil supply came from crude oil refineries, 40 percent from synthetic oil plants and the remainder from other sources such as benzol from coke ovens which, when mixed with gasoline, could be used as a motor fuel. The crude oil passed through fifty-nine major refineries located between Hamburg in Germany and Ploesti, whereas the entire synthetic products output came from plants totally in or quite close to Germany itself.

General Eaker's forces — which included the U.S. 12th and 15th Air Forces, the French Air Force, and the British RAF's Balkan Air Force, Desert Air Force and Coastal Command —

were assigned forty-six crude oil and five synthetic refineries within range of its bombers. Those plants, he estimated, accounted for 60 percent of the entire Axis oil supply, and half of that was in the Ploesti area alone. Production at its eleven refineries—capable of processing more than nine million tons of crude oil annually—had been cut in half by February 1945 through sustained American and British raids in the tough weeks and months of 1944.

Intelligence reports in April 1944—when the 15th Air Force began its Ploesti raids—showed about 150 top-notch German fighter aircraft stationed in Romania whose primary mission was to protect the refineries. In the Ploesti area alone, a ring of 250 heavy flak guns was, in Eaker's words, "one of the largest and certainly among the best coordinated and trained anti-aircraft installations in Europe."

By May and June of that year, the Ploesti defenders had so intensified and improved the smoke pot screen around the refineries that the rising smoke could completely obscure the targets, Eaker said.

The battle of Ploesti began on April 5, 1944, as the Mediterranean Allied Air Forces sought to help the Russian armies advancing on Romania from the east. The first target: the railroad marshalling yards at Ploesti. It was so successful that in subsequent attacks over the next five months the refineries themselves became the primary targets. During that period, the MAAF flew 5,287 sorties (a sortie being one plane flying one mission) over Ploesti and dropped 12,870 tons of bombs.

But Ploesti did not come cheap. Lost were more than 2,200 Americans, shot down and either killed or captured. Half of those men, including Staff Sergeant Harry Fritz, would be brought home in a dramatic and risky rescue mission. The other half never got home. The American forces lost 222 heavy bombers and the British 15. U.S. losses also included ten dive bombers and 39 fighter escorts, many of them in a daring dive bomb attack by thirty-eight P-38 fighters. Little by little that spring and summer Ploesti's oil output was reduced by 60 percent and gasoline exports to the German armed forces were slashed to a third of their previous level.

By August 19, 1944, the Ploesti refineries were in ruins, smashed by an estimated 15,000 tons of bombs. The effect of taking out that complex target was evident in German army orders to Panzer divisions to report each day on gasoline consumption and to use horse-drawn vehicles when possible. All told, about 60,000 Allied airmen (some making more than one run) were involved in raids over that single target. They included B-24 and B-17 crews and the pilots of P-51 Mustang and P-38 Lightning fighters who escorted the bombers to and away from that smoke-filled cauldron of death and destruction. For many, Ploesti was "the toughest target."

The real beginning of the end for Ploesti took place in the summer of 1943 when the second raid occurred. It was codenamed Tidal Wave but has been remembered ever since by those who were there as "the low-level attack." It was approved at a top-secret meeting known as the Casablanca Conference in January of that year. The plan was for 178 B-24 Liberators — each with a ten-man crew — to fly almost 2,700 miles round trip from bases in Africa to Ploesti. The assignment went to five groups from the U.S. 8th and 9th Air Forces. They were told most of the trip would be over enemy territory but that surprise would be a key factor (an expectation which did not come to fruition). They were also told there was no way to provide cover by Allied fighters. To achieve surprise, the planes had to fly low over the Mediterranean, climb over the 10,000-foot peaks of the Yugoslavian mountains, race down the Danube Valley and attack Ploesti from the north. They were ordered to make the bomb run at an altitude under three hundred feet and preferably under one hundred feet, the height of some smoke stacks. It was the only way, planners said, to avoid the German defense warning systems. But it also put the air crews in danger from more guns, including hand-held infantry weapons.

The crews got one last piece of information. It was this: you can expect a third of your planes to be shot down. In fact, one officer predicted a loss of half the planes. At 7:10 a.m. on Sunday, August 1, 1943, the 178 Liberators lifted into the air and began a mission which would result in the awarding of five Medals of Honor, the most for any single military operation in history.[3]

Each plane was carrying a very full load — 3,100 gallons of gasoline plus a full supply of bombs and ammunition. The total weight of 65,000 pounds meant pilots had to struggle to get the heavy planes off the runway. For one the struggle ended on takeoff; it crashed, killing eight of its ten-man crew.

The men who got aloft and started across the Mediterranean had much to think about. They had never flown such a long mission. They had never worked at such a low level, and with smoke from the ground pots or from oil fires visibility would be limited. A bomber flying at more than two hundred miles an hour only one hundred feet above the ground could run into a smoke stack, a building, a hill or another plane. It could also be hit by bullets from a machine gun or even a rifle. It could slam into a cable holding a barrage balloon, and the word was the cables themselves had been fitted with explosive devices.

Their bombs (more than 600,000 pounds for the 178 planes) had time fuses so that deliverers would not be caught in an explosion of their own making. But what of the explosions of bombs dropped by planes far ahead of them in the run to the targets? Would they be caught in those blasts? If there was one bright spot it was that the raid would be on a Sunday when the enemy might be less alert and fewer Romanians and slave laborers would be at work in the refineries. But even that spot disappeared.

Over the sea, ten planes developed engine problems and turned back to their bases. Another, for an unknown reason, turned sideways, plunged into the water and disappeared.

Heavy rain at times caused some pilots to lose sight of other planes and with radio silence in effect they could not call for help. Some flew over heavy cloud cover and some flew under, thus further spreading the formation. By the time they were over the Danube River, mechanical difficulties had forced three more planes to drop out. It took thirteen hours for the remaining bombers to reach Ploesti, but their surprise advantage was lost when they were spotted well before reaching the targets. In addition, spreading of the formation by weather and a serious navigational error by one leader resulted in two groups of bombers attacking from the south and three groups from the north.

Although they encountered neither German nor Romanian fighters on the run in, the raiders did attract heavy flak and small arms fire. Some jettisoned their bombs short of their assigned targets, dumping them in fields and woods outside the refinery ring. Others flew directly into the ring and the city, dodging chimneys and a sky full of lead. Some Liberators were so close to the ground that they shuttered from explosions below them. An entire group was led into its target by a commander who insisted on flying just twenty feet above the ground. One B-24 struck a balloon cable and exploded while another severed a cable without any noticeable effect on board. Some were shot down by roof-top gunners in the city. The pilot of one heavily damaged and doomed bomber apparently decided to do as much damage as possible before crashing. He flew through the walls of one building, came out the other side on fire and without wings, and exploded in mid-air.[4]

Billowing black smoke from exploding oil tanks and white smoke from the pots often prevented pilots from seeing what lay in front of them. One pilot said later that "flights of three or four, or single planes, were flying in different directions, streaking smoke and flames, striking the ground; wings, tails and fuselages breaking up; big balls of smoke rolling out of the wrecks before they stopped shuttering."[5]

Adding to the confusion for the groups approaching from the north was an armored train running at top speed south toward Ploesti and firing anti-aircraft guns at the low-flying planes on both sides of the track. Fixed in their attack formation, the B-24s could change neither course nor altitude. Their only recourse was to fire back at the train.

Over Ploesti, pilots decided their crafts were safer the closer they flew to the ground. One pilot went lower after flak destroyed his hydraulics system, oxygen, electricity and radios. But even hugging the deck brought fire on the attackers. One wave of bombers attacking a refinery went in with six planes but only one emerged still in the air. After the raid, some decided they'd had enough of low-level bombing, leading one pilot to remark that "at 100 feet you see too damn much and, besides being hard on your nerves, it scares hell out of you."[6]

Planes which had dropped their bombs and were exiting the target area skimmed along—as low as twenty feet above ground—to escape enemy fighters waiting for them outside the flak ring. Some, which got home safely, had bits of straw and grass clinging to the fuselage and bomb-bay doors. Many limped back to Africa, taking as long as sixteen hours for the return trip with speed reduced by battle damage. One crew counted 365 shell or bullet holes in their craft.

It was anything but an orderly exit. Liberators were at different altitudes, different speeds, different headings—all governed by their individual situations: damage to the aircraft; wounded pilots; nonfunctioning flight deck instruments; inability to control the plane's movements; an aircraft commander's decision to head for someplace other than the home base; attack by enemy fighters. It was, to say the least, mass confusion.

To avoid fighters, some planes climbed out into cloud cover. For two Liberators that plan did not work. They collided in the swirling fog, and only three of the twenty men aboard survived. In many cases, pilots determined they could not make it back to Africa and took routes toward friendly territory. One headed for Turkey and crashed into the Black Sea just a half mile from shore. The impact jammed escape hatches but the fuselage was so weakened by shell hits that seven crewmen were able to batter their way out through the metal walls before the plane sank.

Of the 177 B-24s that had successfully taken off the day before, only 111 returned to their bases and more than half of those were badly damaged. Forty-one planes were lost in action—to fighters, to flak, to other guns. Eight had landed in Turkey and were confiscated by officials there. Five had crashed due to unknown causes. The Germans and Romanians lost twelve fighters and had twenty damaged.

The fifty-four American planes lost had carried 542 men, of whom 298 were killed. In addition, 150 wounded and unwounded crewmen were taken prisoner in Romania and Bulgaria, 75 were interned in Turkey and 19 were rescued from downed bombers. Even some of the crewmen whose planes made it back to Africa joined the casualty list; more than fifty survived the round trip only to die or be disabled by their wounds. One bomber took sixteen hours to limp back to its base; it had two engines out, had no hydraulic power, and had no instrument lights to make a night landing easier.

It took months to fully assess the effectiveness of Tidal Wave. Initial reports claimed great success. However, by the following spring it was determined that while the raid caused very heavy damage it did not deliver a knockout blow. By October 1943, the Ploesti refineries were processing more crude oil than they did the month before the raid. But then, no one had ever predicted that one raid would remove Ploesti from the target list.

Tidal Wave did prove at least one theory: that Allied airbases had to be closer to the targets and that fighter escort to and away from the refineries was mandatory. It also showed that a prolonged flight by too many bombers created too many problems en route.

Three weeks after the attack, American target analysts reasoned that the "most important effect was to eliminate the cushion between production and capacity" of the Ploesti refineries. In other words, Hitler was still getting the oil products he needed at that period. But the war was changing and the dictator desperately needed that extra cushion of oil to battle the British and Americans on two new fronts in Italy and Russian movements to the east.

In July, the Allies invaded Sicily and by August 17 they occupied all of that island. Within weeks, British and Canadian troops of the 8th Army jumped across to the Boot of Italy. They were followed on September 9 when the U.S. 5th Army — sailing from Africa — landed at Salerno some two hundred miles up the west coast of Italy. The 8th struggled up the Boot, fighting a tough 400,000-man German force but gaining ground slowly through the mud and winter cold. By late 1943, the Germans were pushed far enough north to allow Allied airmen to establish the bases they needed on the heel of the Italian Boot along the Adriatic Sea.

The 15th Air Force found it was a slow go from Africa to Europe. There was a delay in getting material for the buildings it would need in Italy to house crews and offices and kitchens. It took time to rebuild the captured airfields, which were too small for American bombers, and even longer to build new runways. Much of the problem was due to wintry weather. Christmas had come and gone before all of the heavy bombers were moved from Tunisia to Foggia and other sites in Italy. Tunisian bases were then transformed into receiving areas for new bombers and their crews arriving from the United States.

The buildup in Italy was gradual, with selected numbers of aircraft and men scheduled to arrive each month. For example, the December-January allocation was 739 B-24s with 937 crews and 200 B-17s with 178 crews. The plan from then on was to bring in 171 B-24s with 217 crews and 60 B-17s with 87 crews monthly.

From the new bases astride the Adriatic atop the Italian Boot, it was now only five hundred miles across that sea, over Yugoslavia and to Ploesti. Once again, Ploesti strike plans were on the front burner. But it took until April 1944 before a buildup of aircraft, crews, ammunition, aviation fuel, and other supplies was sufficient to make the trip worthwhile.

Tidal Wave also had another important effect. "The First of August aroused stirrings of national spirit, and Romania began a slow upturn from resignation to active resistance toward the Nazis."[7]

The die was cast.

1 ⟩ FROM VILLAGE TO WAR

The doomed American bomber was down to six thousand feet above enemy territory when Staff Sergeant Harry Fritz bailed out through the small hatch in the B-24's belly, whisked away from the whirling wash of the plane's remaining two engines, and pulled his rip cord. He had marked his twenty-first birthday just three weeks earlier and now wondered if he would survive to celebrate his twenty-second.

He had never set foot anywhere in Europe, except at his base in the Italian Boot, but now was floating over Romania alone — for he could see no other parachutes — and frightened.

In the past year, he had traveled more than he had in his entire life, had seen more of the United States than he ever would again, had flown across the Atlantic in his first long air trip, and had experienced the terror of war from the tail gunner's position on the Liberator.

It was certainly not what he expected! Like others fighting in World War II, he tried to convince himself that it was always the other guy who died.

He was a long way from the small village of Pine Grove near the bottom end of the huge anthracite mine fields of eastern Pennsylvania. Graduation with thirty-nine classmates from Pine Grove High School in June 1942 was now a distant memory. In fact, everything about his past seemed just a blur as he floated over forests and farm fields.

After graduation, he car-pooled with four others for an hour each way every day to attend an aeronautics repair school and work as a fuselage mechanic's helper at the Middletown Air Depot near Harrisburg, the state capital. He had been there six months when the letter he knew would come from the draft board back home arrived. The notice told him to report for a physical examination the day after Christmas 1942. It was a routine notice. Everyone he knew of his generation in Pine Grove was getting the same letter. As a healthy nineteen-year-old there was no question he would pass. It would be, he thought, embarrassing not to pass, not to go, not to serve. It was expected of young men that they would defend their country. It was part of the lesson taught by good citizens like his parents, Bruce and Lillian Fritz, both school teachers. His father was a native Pennsylvanian from Columbia County just to the north and his mother was of pioneer stock from North Dakota. Harry was the lone boy in a family of five children. One of the girls was his twin.

When orders arrived to report for active duty on February 16, 1943, there was a hitch. Fritz was in the hospital, recovering from an appendectomy. It took letters from his father and his physician to convince the army he couldn't go, at least not then. The revised orders gave a sixty-day delay. By the time everything was rearranged, summer was fast approaching. On June 4, Harry Fritz — still a teenager — was inducted at New Cumberland, just across the broad Susquehanna River from Harrisburg.

He had never been far from home before, hardly out of Pennsylvania in fact. But that summer he found himself at Gulfport Field in Mississippi, along with hundreds of other army recruits. Basic training had always been an adventure which old boys and young men saw as their passage to true manhood. It was that way for him too.

After boot camp, he was sent to Lowry Field near Denver, Colorado, for airplane armorers school conducted by the Army Air Force. He learned how to disassemble and reassemble a jammed .55 caliber gun—blindfolded. He learned how to wire the bombs in a plane's bomb bay. Most of all he learned how to operate and fix the ten machine guns on a standard B-24. Each of the turrets—tail, nose, top and belly or ball—had two guns while the waist gunners had one apiece. In addition to being one of the gunners, his auxiliary duty on board would be as the armorer. Each bomber had an armorer. In fact, every gunner on board would have an extra job in addition to fighting off enemy air attacks.

From Denver, then Private First Class Harry B. Fritz was transferred to Amarillo, Texas, for training from the rear cockpit seat of an AT-6, an aircraft used to train fighter pilots and aerial gunners. Hanging on to the fuselage he was told to partially stand in the seat to feel the violent push of the slip stream. And from the seat he learned to fire a .30 caliber machine gun at a sleeve towed by another plane. That training was augmented on the ground by putting future gunners in the back of a speeding pickup truck. Armed with shotguns they fired at clay pigeons. "They taught us how to lead a target while moving ourselves," he said.

Fritz by now was getting used to flying. He

So-called nose art decorated many aircraft in World War II. Here, Staff Sergeant Fritz poses in front of one B-24 tagged as "The Lively Lady."

Harry Fritz Collection

was sent to the Army Air Forces Flexible Gunnery School at Harlingen Army Air Field in Texas where someone told him in confidence that if he purposely flunked out he could avoid flying in combat. There would be none of that, Fritz decided. He completed the course and was promoted to corporal. A press release from the army to his hometown newspaper said that along with his diploma he received his aerial gunner's wings. It continued: "Corporal Fritz was prepared for his place in America's stepped-up air offensive by a comprehensive six weeks course in every phase of aerial gunnery warfare. Besides learning to fire every type of weapon from camera guns to the deadly caliber .50 Brownings, he studied turret manipulation and aircraft identification, and learned to tear down and assemble machine guns while blindfolded. He climaxed the course by firing on towed targets from Texas training planes, medium bombers and Liberators."

From Texas he went to Westover Field near Springfield, Massachusetts, ostensibly to meet with other crew members from a plane to which he would be assigned. The cross-country trip gave him the first chance to visit home since boot camp, a welcome ten-day respite from all of the mandatory training to prepare him for duty in a bomber crew. Three weeks passed at Westover and no crew meeting took place. It was a quiet three weeks after the hectic schedule of training camps and schools but it was an important time in his life. At a USO dance there he met a girl who, in 1948, would become Mrs. Harry B. Fritz.

The army then sent him to Chatham Field near Savannah, Georgia, for specialized training. It included two flights to Cuba, more suited for pilots and navigators to experience flying over large bodies of water than anyone else on board, but all crewmen had to go. On these longer flights he and his crewmates became well aware of the tightness inside a B-24. To enter, the navigator, bombardier and nose gunner squeezed up through the hole where the nose wheel was stored in flight and took positions in a cramped compartment in front of and below the cockpit. The rest of the crew pulled themselves up through the open bomb bay doors and moved on a narrow catwalk to the cockpit, to the radioman's post just behind and below the copilot, or to the other gun positions.

Fritz now had a grand total of eighty-three hours and fifteen minutes in training time aboard B-24s, and the longest he had been aloft was six hours and forty-five minutes. He found that when sitting in the tail with his feet sticking down into the turret he barely had room to move and certainly had no room to wear a parachute.

The trips to Cuba were his first long flights in the B-24 and he quickly learned that the standard loaded Liberator weighed 30 to 35 tons, had a wing span of 110 feet, a length of 66 feet and a height of 18 feet. With its four 1,200-horsepower engines, it could hit top speed of just over 300 miles per hour, reach an altitude of 28,000 feet and normally fly 2,100 miles without refueling. He also learned several names used by airmen to describe a B-24, among them "pregnant cow," "banana boat," and "flying box car," all apparently related to the plane's appearance. Although it looked strong enough, crewmen were concerned that the plane's aluminum covering was thin enough to break through with a hammer or cut through with a big knife. Design work on the Consolidated B-24 began in 1939 and by 1941 the aircraft was in service. During World War II more B-24s were built than any other combat plane in the American arsenal—a total of 18,432.

There were no heaters inside the craft, even though temperatures at bombing altitudes above 20,000 feet could fall to 50 degrees below zero. And the wind which seeped through openings such as the bomb bay doors and waist gun openings made the cold almost unbearable. At times, the waist gunners and the men in the ball turret and tail turret would be covered with frost. Oxygen masks—necessary above 10,000 feet because bombers were not pressurized—often froze, making it impossible for the wearer to remove it. "You quickly learned never to touch metal inside the plane with your bare skin," Fritz recalled.

Each crewman wore an electrically heated flight suit, including soft boots and gloves. But if the plane's electrical system failed then the suits were almost useless. So in addition, they had heavy leather pants, coats, hats and gloves lined with sheepskin, which Fritz said they seldom wore because the outfits were too bulky in the B-24's tight quarters.

There was no equipment to warm up food or drinks. There were no toilets. Urinating meant using one of two small tubes on board, which themselves were often plugged with frozen urine. Defecating was in a waxed paper bag, if one was brave enough to chance having bare skin accidentally touch bare metal or simply be exposed to frostbite. There was no floor as we know it in a modern aircraft; rather, crewman moved along the narrow catwalk which took them between the bombs and over the bomb bay doors. And care was needed, for the weight of a falling man was enough to break through the fragile doors.

Later, in Europe, he would hear pilots complain about how difficult it was to get the Liberator with a complete crew, normal bomb load, ammunition and full gas tanks off the runway. Consolidated Aircraft, which built the B-24, said the maximum takeoff weight for the bomber was sixty-three thousand pounds, but for bombing missions the planes were usually overloaded by eight thousand pounds. When pilots questioned the safety factor they were asked: "What do you want to leave behind?" For a successful mission they knew there was nothing they could leave behind. "It seemed as though we were flying just above the ground for the longest time after takeoff," Fritz said. The pilots also talked about how tough it was on a man's arms just to steer a Liberator and how wrong it was to attempt a crash-landing at sea. War records show that only a fourth of the Liberators which tried water landings stayed afloat long enough for the crew to get out. And those drawbacks did not even include the biggest danger: getting shot down or forced down over enemy territory.

Eastern theater of operations for the 15th Air Force, based in southern Italy by the end of 1943, included this section of Europe, plus France to the west.
Map prepared by Jonathan G. Williams; drawn by Jim Robinson

Word had filtered back from England — where the U.S. 8th Air Force was in action and the required tour of duty was twenty-five missions — that loss rates meant, theoretically, that no airmen would survive to complete a tour. In fact, by 1943, bomber losses in Europe were so heavy that it could be argued a crewman would have difficulty in even completing thirteen missions. Later, when Allied bomber crews got better fighter protection and German fighter pilots and planes became fewer, the mission number for a crewman would rise to thirty-five and then fifty. That knowledge alone gave little hope for new airmen leaving the States for combat duty.

Fritz's last stop was Mitchell Field, New York, an embarkation center for crews leaving U.S. shores for war theater assignments. He was a staff sergeant now, the required minimum rank for bomber crewmen, and the designated tail gunner.

There was a valid reason for making sure that each airman who would be in European combat was at least a staff sergeant. It had everything to do with Hermann Goering, commander of Hitler's Luftwaffe. The Army Air Force learned early in the war that the Germans treated captured Allied sergeants better than corporals or privates and also that Allied airmen were interned in prison camps run by the Luftwaffe, not by the army or the Gestapo. Goering, a World War I fighter ace, appreciated the efforts and talents of those who fought from the sky and so ordered that his prison camps be better than the ones that held foot soldiers. The natural conclusion of the American air commanders was simply that every man flying in combat over German territory would rank no lower than staff sergeant.

At Key West, Florida, Fritz finally met the other crewmen and saw the B-24 they would fly to Europe. The next day, his pilot told every crewman — even the gunners — to check the fuel supply. "He told every one of us to take off the caps and look into the tanks. He wanted to make sure we all agreed the tanks were full," Fritz said.

When Staff Sergeant Fritz and nine other airmen lifted off from American soil and headed east they knew that the next stop would be in West Africa. It brought moments of concern. Cross the Atlantic?

Even though they had all checked the tanks they still wondered if there was sufficient fuel for such a long haul. American bombers had been doing it for two years, though there had been accidents. Like all airmen, the crew wondered about the capability of their navigator to locate their destination and their pilot to guide the big bomber safely in.

Only the pilot, copilot, navigator and engineer were needed to get the plane and crew across the ocean. The bombardier and gunners had no function on this trip. They were passengers, able only to lie or sit on the metal deck in the waist of the crammed fuselage. There were no hot meals nor a toilet.

This B-24, number 618, carried Staff Sergeant Fritz and fellow crewmen from America to the war in Europe.

Staff Sergeant Fritz poses beneath the Plexiglas canopy of his tail-gun position.

They had time to sleep, or talk, or read, or worry, but nothing to do. Though they couldn't see land they knew they would be flying over the Bahamas and just north of Cuba. Within two hours and some five hundred miles from Florida's east coast they would slide by Haiti and its island neighbor, the Dominican Republic, sidestep Puerto Rico and then the Lesser Antilles before rushing over the vast expanse of the Atlantic separating the Caribbean from Africa.

The destination was Dakar, the capital of Senegal, on the Cape Verde peninsula, part of the French West Africa community. The crew was relieved when—eight hours after take-off from Florida—the B-24 lumbered into the airfield, safely across the big pond but now within the war zone. It was an overnight stop, sleeping in a tent with no chance to see the local scenery, to get a feel for Africa or its inhabitants.

The next day they were airborne again, heading north-east en route to Tunis, another capital city and the chief port of Tunisia on the north coast of the African continent. They were now in the center of what had been the North African Campaign area in 1942 and 1943 before Allied forces pushed German and Italian troops across the Mediterranean and back into Europe. They were also in the middle of the great Sahara Desert, three and a half million square miles of sand, the world's largest desert. It caused concern because a plane downed in that vast wasteland could be lost forever.

Tunis was special because it was the last refueling stop before a hop across the Mediterranean to their base on the heel of the Italian Boot. It was also where the crew learned the phrase "mix with water and stir" when they were introduced to dehydrated food. They would fly on the next day to a 15th Air Force base in southern Italy, or so they thought.

The airfield at Tunis, like most bases in any area fought over by World War II troops, was constantly undergoing repairs. There were fifty-gallon metal drums in the strangest places, including some on the runway along which Fritz's plane was rolling for takeoff early the next morning. "We hit some of those drums, the nose wheel collapsed and we skidded to a quick stop," Fritz recalls. "We were scared and frustrated at the same time." When the plane's nose hit the runway the tail shot up in the air, giving Fritz the highest seat of the entire crew. He had to crawl downhill to get to the waist belly escape hatch.

After safely crossing the Atlantic and the Sahara, the crew wondered if the crash on their last leg was a bad omen or just poor runway maintenance. It didn't matter. Their plane was unable to go on, but the crew, shaken though not injured, was. They were shuttled by air to Italy the next day and assigned to a base near the town of Foggia, eighty miles northeast of Naples and seventy miles northwest of the 15th Air Force headquarters at Bari, a city at the top of the heel on the Italian Boot. Another B-24 for fighting and Quonset huts for living were waiting for them.

They were now part of the 513th Bomb Squadron, 376th Bomb Group, 47th Wing, 15th Air Force. The 47th Wing was the first complete wing in that theater of the war but sixteen more would join them soon. The 47th had four groups—the 376th, the 98th (which had taken part in the August 1, 1943, low-level raid on the massive oil refineries at Ploesti, Romania), the 449th and the 450th.

Fritz and his crew had arrived. They would soon be airborne again for their first mission. For them the war had arrived too.

2 ▷ DEATH ON THE FIRST RUN

There was time at Foggia only for the necessities—getting assigned to a bunk in a Quonset hut, filling out the paperwork always required by the military in order to keep track of its men, and preparing mentally for war.

Foggia had been captured by British troops in October 1943 and was surrounded by former Axis airfields, now all in Allied hands. The 15th Air Force was under the command of Major General James Doolittle—who in 1942 had led the first bombing raid on Tokyo—when it began moving from Africa to the Italian Boot in November. Three weeks before Christmas it opened its new headquarters at Bari. In January, Doolittle was transferred to England where he took command of the 8th Air Force.

One of the first tasks in Italy was repair of the runways which the 15th itself had damaged when the airfields were occupied by German and Italian forces. Some of the runways were then paved or overlaid with steel mesh to keep the heavy bombers from sinking into the mud. The work crews even laid pipelines to pump gasoline for the aircraft from the headquarters at Bari to the fields around Foggia.

Like the others, Fritz had experienced formation flying during his stateside training. Huge bombers flown by men with little or no flying experience before they became part of the U.S. Army Air Corps were bunched together in combat boxes to practice techniques which, hopefully, would give them some protection from fast and deadly enemy fighter aircraft. It was virtually wing tip to wing tip, the closer the better. Go in like a wedge, pushing through the fighters; using the bottom planes to fight off attacks from below, the top planes to defend the diving assaults from above, the outside edges protecting the formation from head-on or from the rear or from the sides. Protect the formation from all angles, they were taught. When you close on the target and encounter shards of steel from the flak guns, the fighter planes will back away, but they'll be waiting again once your bombs are dropped and you're heading home.

A bomber group normally had thirty-six planes, plus a few spares, divided into four squadrons. The procedure called for getting the bombers into formation over the home field. Three planes were usually on the runway at one time: the first just lifting off the ground, the second halfway through its run, the third releasing its brakes to start the run. Even at that quick pace, it could take an hour to get the formation properly aligned while flying in circles at three thousand feet above the field.

A normal combat box would have between eighteen and twenty-one bombers in each group. A combat wing included three such groups: the lead group out front; the second group one thousand feet higher and off to one side; the third group one thousand feet lower and off to the other side. Thus, with ten machine guns per B-24, a wing of fifty-four bombers would present a formidable challenge with well over five hundred guns facing enemy fighters. There were variations on the boxes, depending on the number of planes attacking a target. For example, a squadron box might have seven B-24s in two three-plane patterns, one forty feet behind and below the other, with a lone bomber following the lower group. With four squadrons in a group, the protective screen would be divided into a lead box, a high box, a low box and a middle box.

Fighter pilots on both sides knew the problems involved in attacking such a bomber formation. They knew they had only seconds to fire off a few rounds before their speed sent them racing past the tightly packed formation. They knew that from any angle, a multitude of gunners from a number of bombers would be lining them up in their sights. They knew that only one bullet hitting their single engine or a gas tank could be enough to send them spiraling down in flames or exploding in the air. It was not easy for them to get close enough to shoot down or disable a bomber, but they would gain the skills needed to do just that or they would on occasion just get lucky.

Enemy gunners on the ground also used the box system to blast planes out of the sky. As the bombers approached and the Germans determined their altitude, the ground crews would set their shells to explode at that altitude. Then, instead of each gun picking a target, they simply all fired into a specific area of the sky to create a box of explosions as the planes flew through. Shells from heavy anti-aircraft weapons would throw out hundreds of shrapnel pieces that could kill anything within thirty feet.

There had been accidents during training, and crewmen died, but Fritz had not personally seen any crashes in the States, only read or heard of them. Reading or hearing of fatal accidents was an exercise in statistics; actually seeing them was a lesson in horror.

His crew's first mission briefing came at 5 a.m., the normal time bomber crews assembled to learn where they'd be going and what they'd be hitting. Reveille was at 4 a.m. Breakfast of fresh food and lots of coffee followed, the last meal crews would have until they returned, often eight, or ten, or twelve hours later. There was neither food nor drink on the aircraft.

Wood's Chopper was the name given to this B-24, whose navigator was First Lieutenant Donald R. Currier. At the instant this photo was taken from another B-24 en route to a bombing mission, the tailgunner was testing his guns (white smoke barely visible).

Courtesy of Colonel Donald R. Currier, USAF-Retired

The veterans at Foggia, as at all American bases, could tell the newcomers about targets they had visited before but they could never fully explain the feeling of leaving their runway, perhaps never to return; or what flak really looked and sounded like; or the sudden terror of an enemy fighter zipping by so suddenly and so closely that the pilot's face was sometimes visible for a split second. Most didn't even try. They didn't really want to recall their own brushes with death nor did they want to put that fear into the hearts of newcomers.

At briefings, crewmen first learned the target for the day. It could be east, or north, or west—hundreds upon hundreds of miles away—a factory or a submarine pen—a so-called "milk run" or a mission destined to bring heavy losses. For pilots, copilots, navigators and bombardiers the emphasis was on the route of travel, distance, altitude of the formation, cloud cover or rain or other weather information, and most of all, the target. Bombing would be from high altitudes, generally above twenty thousand feet. Anything above ten thousand required oxygen masks and heated flight suits.

Fritz was twenty years old when he was shaken from a deep sleep on that first mission day. No one said much as they dressed in the light thermal suits and socklike boots required for high flight in an unheated aircraft where wind whipped through the fuselage. It was still dark as he walked with his buddies to the mess hall and ate what he could while thinking about what that day would bring.

The mission destination was Toulon, a seaport of some 100,000 people on the Mediterranean coast of France. The target: a German navy submarine base. Flying time: eight hours to target and return.

The flak would be moderate, the briefing officer predicted, though Fritz (and no doubt others) had no idea of what that relative term meant. Was "moderate flak" nothing to worry about? Was "moderate flak" fired too low to hit the bombers? Was "moderate flak" just as deadly as light flak or heavy flak if it struck your aircraft? There would always be questions, and each man, over time, would form in his own mind which degrees of flak he had encountered on each mission.

Daylight was breaking as the bomber crews loaded themselves through the tight entrances into the thin metal box that would be their home for a good part of that day. The four officers—like the rest of the crew just barely out of their teenage years—were up front: pilot and copilot on the highest level, navigator and bombardier just a few feet below. The six staff sergeants included: the engineer, who assisted the pilots by watching the aircraft instruments; the nose gunner up in his forward bubble; the top turret man, who stood on a shelf with his head in a circular Plexiglas roof; the ball turret gunner, always by necessity a small man who could fold up inside the ball underneath the plane; the waist gunner, who took the brunt of cold air blasts through the windowless openings on both sides of the fuselage; and the tailgunner, back by himself and seated between the Liberator's twin tails. Earlier in the war, such bombers had carried two waist gunners. While every other crew member could see where the plane was going, either through a window or a side opening, the tailgunner could only see where the plane had been.

A B-17 Flying Fortress, *at left*, and a B-24 Liberator return together to Italy from a bombing raid.

Part of a B-24 formation en route to a target. Many more planes would be above, below and on all sides in a tight grouping. The tail gunner is seated in the transparent pod between the twin tails.

The pilots—strapped into metal seats designed to protect them from flak coming through the thin skin of the plane's bottom—wore back parachutes. The others had chest packs and donned them only when there was a chance they'd have to bail out. Fritz found he didn't have room to wear a parachute when seated at his gun behind the Plexiglas shield. Neither did most of the others. Besides, who wanted to think the day would come when they'd have to jump to avoid riding a dead plane into the ground? Fritz also found that he could not maneuver in that tight tail bubble with the bulky coat, pants, boots and gloves. He preferred to just plug in his electric suit and sock-boots to keep warm.

On the ground, officers and enlisted personnel kept their distance to some extent, neither sleeping nor eating in the same building, seldom socializing, no first names used, no buddy-buddy, no time off spent together. It was and is the military way of instilling discipline. It meant salutes and "sir" and proper respect for those in command.

In the air, it was different. "The crew was family, even with the officers," Fritz says. "The pilot was in charge but he treated all crewmen as family. In combat, the officers were your friends, not your superiors." They would fly together, fight together, survive together. All depended on each other to return from a mission. All knew they had a special responsibility to keep the aircraft flying, to keep the men living. Four hours to Toulon this first day, four hours back. Everyone had a job to do!

The bombers left the runway in close order, much too close for what would be considered safe in today's commercial aviation. The first task was gathering in formations, in boxes of protective cover that would aim many .50 caliber machine guns at enemy fighters. Depending on the number of planes going on a mission it could take an hour for all to lift off, climb to the assigned altitude, and circle until each could join the formation in a pre-assigned position. Like most maneuvers at that time, just forming up could be dangerous. And it was on Fritz's first mission.

"We were still circling, forming up," Fritz recalled. "Only five planes were in the formation when, suddenly, two of them came together. That's all it took, just coming together, just touching. There was a flash, an explosion and both planes fell. There were no parachutes, no survivors. Twenty men died in an instant, before the mission even got started."

But the mission went on. Gunners tested their weapons by firing short bursts. Pilots and copilots concentrated on staying dangerously close to other planes in their box. Navigators depended on the navigator in the first plane to lead them to the target, but they still had to keep track of their route in case, just in case, engine problems forced them to turn back alone. The bombardier, engineer and radioman prepared themselves to handle whatever developed during the long ride in. But there were still four hours of little activity before Toulon to think about what they had all witnessed, the loss of two planes and their crews over their home base. For Fritz and the other nine aboard his B-24 it was a frightening introduction to war.

And they hadn't seen it all, not yet. The second shock would come over the sub pens at Toulon—a sky seemingly filled with red splotches from the explosion of shells, black smoke patching the sky and the knowledge that lethal chunks of metal were flying about them. They had their first view of deadly flak.

If the German gunners had figured correctly on the formation's altitude they could set their shells to explode at that altitude. Two things were certain when bombers entered the flak zone—one bad, one good. First, no friendly fighters would escort them through. Second, no enemy fighters would be there either. There was nothing a friendly fighter pilot could do to protect a bomber from flak and he—like the enemy pilot—only put himself and his airplane in jeopardy by flying through flak. But the bombers had to fly through the black hell which enveloped targets.

The third scare for Fritz's plane of newcomers arrived when trouble—for whatever reason—developed in the number three engine. Immediately, the pilot feathered the prop by pressing a cockpit button to stop the propeller from windmilling and thus slowing the Liberator's speed. A slow bomber, unable to keep up with its formation and the protection it afforded, could become a sitting duck for skilled German fighter pilots. The four-engine Liberators—labeled by some crews as "flying coffins"—lost too much power when two engines were out.

This first day ended in success: mission completed; target hit; the aircraft only slightly damaged; crew uninjured; safe landing at home. And, the veteran crewmen said, the briefing officer was right; the flak was moderate. But some of it had hit Fritz's plane. In fact, on every mission he flew, his plane took at least one and often several hits from flak or enemy fighter guns.

Fritz would find in the missions which lay ahead that he wasn't alarmed about the trip to the target, despite the fact that he—like many others—had always been afraid of heights. "There was too much on my mind to worry, too many other things to think about. Your mind was always occupied. On the way out I test fired my guns and then watched for fighters."

Over the target there was nothing for him or the other gunners to do but watch the bombing run or see to their auxiliary duties. It was Fritz's secondary job, as the plane's armorer, to make sure all the guns were working properly. On the run out of the flak area all crewmen were on the lookout for German fighters and reporting their location to the aircraft's gunners in the tail and nose, above and below and on the sides. The tailgunner could see what others in the crew couldn't; so could the ball turret gunner slung beneath the fuselage.

Once safely out of the range of those fighters, "we just sat" for the ride back to base, Fritz said of the gunners and the

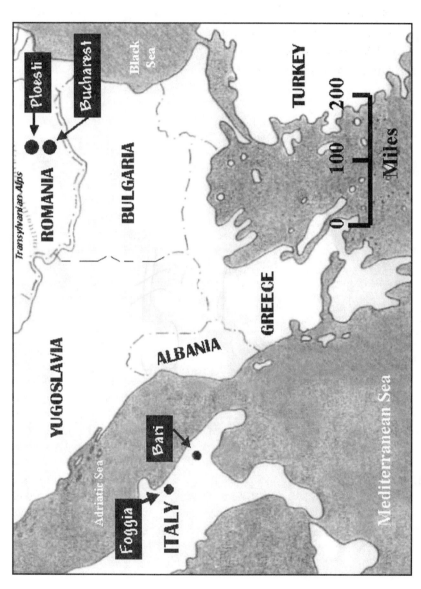

The 15th Air Force headquarters base was at Bari in southern Italy; Sergeant Fritz was based at Foggia. One of their toughest targets was the ring of oil refineries which surrounded the city of Ploesti, Romania.

Map by Jonathan G. Williams

bombardier. On this day, the first day for this crew, the safe homecoming was tempered by the knowledge that twenty men and two aircraft were still in smoldering ruins on the ground below them. Two crews destined for that mission would never fly in this life again. It was an ending repeated time and time again for airmen the world over.

3 ◇ A MISSION EVERY DAY

The very next day, Fritz and his crew were on the schedule again. Up at 4 a.m., breakfast, briefing at 5, checking gear, climbing aboard — the same routine.

The target was a railroad bridge being used by the Germans to move troops and equipment. The flight would take at least six hours, cover nine hundred miles round trip and be subjected to flak and possibly fighters.

They were going to Tagliamento, Italy, a town about fifty miles northwest of Trieste and forty miles northeast of Venice. The route was mostly over the waters of the Adriatic, relatively free of enemy attack until they neared land. At the extreme northern end of the Adriatic they cleared the coast and flew less than twenty miles inland to the target. Despite their close proximity the airmen would not see Trieste — a port city at the head of that ancient sea and until 1920 a part of the Hapsburg Empire — nor the fabled and watery Venice. Trieste and Venice were just two of many historic sites across Europe which Allied airmen would never see at ground level unless they returned after the war.

It was a very clear day, ideal for precision bombing in the days before an improved bomb sight was available. "The hit was perfect," Fritz remembers. The bridge was put out of commission. No German fighters came up to challenge the raid. And, best of all, the flak was "light."

There was no letup for the squadron. When the weather was decent, the bombers flew. And when the weather was decent every day, the bombers flew every day. Each mission brought something new, something to write in a diary (which really was against regulations) or stick in one's memory.

For the third day in a row, Fritz's plane was ticketed for another raid. This one was going to a target near Zagreb in Yugoslavia, about one hundred miles east of Trieste, Italy, where they'd been the day before. The route was almost directly north, about half over the Adriatic and half over western Yugoslavia. The round trip was tabbed at almost eight hundred miles, six hours of flight time.

Briefing officers had some good news: American fighters would provide an escort for the Liberators. The bomb run would be from 22,000 feet and flak was expected to be light. Fritz, with just two missions under his belt, was still uncertain how briefers could determine the degree of flak, even if a target had been hit before. Would not the Germans increase the number of flak guns around a target which had been hit before and thereby offer medium flak or heavy flak? He did not know the answer. But he did know that flak of any intensity was a hazard. If it hits your plane you could be wounded or killed or doomed to ride the crippled aircraft to the ground. If it misses, well, there's always tomorrow.

Two things went wrong on this Zagreb mission:

First, Fritz said, "some trigger-happy gunner" in a B-24 took a shot at one of the escort fighters—by accident, it was assumed. Fortunately, he missed.

Second, the lead plane for some unexplained reason erred and the location of the target was missed. In such situations when no secondary target was available or when weather prevented bombardiers from seeing any targets, the bombs were not carried back to base. It was much too dangerous to land with bombs which could bounce loose and explode. So each plane jettisoned its lethal cargo, over water if possible, over land if necessary.

Even though the bombers missed their target, the German gunners at Zagreb did not hold back. Up came the flak and, like the briefing officer predicted, it was light.

Early the following morning, the crews were awakened again — the fourth day in a row but a much different day than the other three. They would be going further north, further into German territory, beyond Italy, past Yugoslavia.

Staff Sergeant Fritz displays his insulated flight suit and front parachute.
Harry Fritz Collection

And they were told they would get double credit for this mission; that is, it would count as two missions in their quest for the magic number of thirty-five missions that would send them home.

The targets were aircraft hangars at a German base near Markersdorf, Austria. The base was well defended but it had become necessary to strike solid blows at the enemy's capability to put fighter planes up against Allied bombers. It was labeled a dangerous mission, thus the double credit. Once again, the bombing altitude would be 22,000 feet. There would be fighter escorts.

On the run in, the lead aircraft could not see the target. Everyone followed as the leader made a wide sweep and prepared to make a second run. From his seat in the tail, Fritz could only see where they had been, not where they were going. He was watching for ME-109s, his finger on the trigger of his .50 caliber gun. What he saw brought back flashes of his first mission, just a few days earlier. Two of the Liberators were hit and were going down. One exploded before his eyes. He saw only two parachutes blossoming out behind him, two out of a possible twenty.

The weather stayed good and the daily grind went on. The following morning's briefing brought an ominous word which echoed throughout the room: Ploesti. It had a reputation which extended back to 1942 and particularly to a murderous low-level raid by 156 B-24s in August 1943. It was considered one of the three most dangerous targets in the entire European Theater of Operations. It too was worth a double mission count for those who survived. The city of Ploesti in eastern Romania was surrounded by eleven huge oil refineries which provided a third of the oil needed by Germany to wage war. They had been hit many times but still stood, still produced gigantic amounts of oil products, still thumbed their collective smokestacks at American and British bombers which had been trying to grind them into dust.

After the single 1943 raid, Ploesti had not been attacked again until April 5, 1944, when the 15th Air Force had the planes and the crews to stage a major operation. On that April day, 230 bombers struck the oil refineries. One of the young navigators on that raid, and on raids to come, was Donald R. Currier, who would later say: "Attacking Ploesti was as close to visiting hell as one could imagine." The 15th came back ten days later and again on April 24. The heat was being applied to Hitler's main oil supply. On May 5, Currier wrote in his book, 50 Mission Crush, the 15th made a "maximum effort" by hitting both the Ploesti refineries and the marshalling yards in one raid. They didn't knock out the facilities "but we gave it a heck of a shot." Currier said there were sixteen groups in two bomber streams on that raid, some five hundred heavy bombers.

While Allied troops were storming ashore at Normandy on June 6, the 15th flew to Ploesti again, followed by raids on

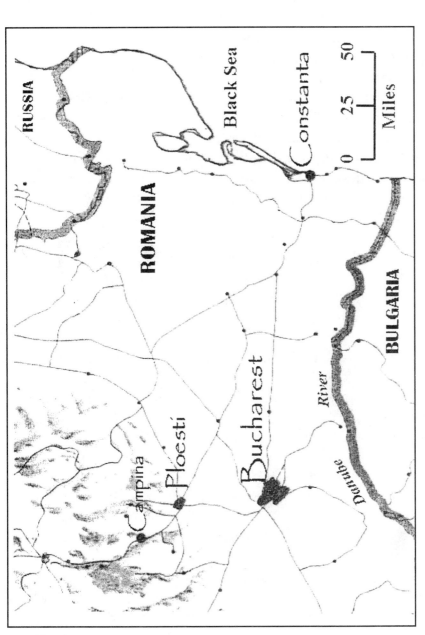

Oil-rich refinery city of Ploesti, *at left*, was the target of major air raids into Romania. To the south is Bucharest, site of a German/Romanian prisoner-of-war camp which was liberated by the U.S. Army Air Force.

Map by Jonathan G. Williams

June 23 and 24, and on July 9 and 15. But the attacks came at a high price, costing the 15th Air Force forty-six bombers on the two July missions alone. Between April 5 and July 15, the unit lost ninety bombers, just over Ploesti, and numerous others in raids elsewhere.

The commander of the United States Strategic Air Forces had had enough. Lieutenant General Carl Spaatz convinced the supreme Allied commander, Dwight Eisenhower, that the main target of the 8th and 15th Air Forces had to be oil refineries, not bridges and trains. On June 8, Spaatz ordered the two units to focus mainly on denying oil to the Nazi machine. From that point on, Ploesti and other oil refineries became the primary targets.

Ploesti! The name alone was enough to strike terror. It had taken a large toll of airplanes and air crews. Today would be a shot for Fritz and his crew, another attempt to close the spigot which kept Hitler's planes and ships and tanks and trucks rolling. The escort going in and coming out would be P-51s. The altitude for "bombs away" would be slightly higher at 24,000 feet, still well within the range of mammoth flak guns. For the first time, Fritz found out what it meant to fly through heavy flak.

But the mission was a bust. The oil fields were dotted with large smoke pots which even blotted out the sun for those on the ground. From above it was impossible to see the ground. And, on this day — this day especially — radar equipment in the lead plane making the run at one of the refineries failed to work. No runs, no hits, one error and a safe return to home base.

In just five days, Fritz and his buddies had flown five missions with credit earned for seven. So far they had come back safely, though always with a few new holes in the wings or the fuselage from the sharp fragments of metal fired aloft by the flak guns or from a fighter's machine gun bullets. And, so far, no one, at least on his plane, had been wounded.

Four memories were etched into his mind in those five missions: the importance of good visibility for a successful bomb run; that the bombardier was the key person on the run in to the target; that flak was the biggest problem for the bombers; and that even close flak blasts which missed striking an aircraft could bounce it up and down.

Those facts of combat life were strong among bomber crews, but there was a fifth consideration too, one which had nothing to do with winning or losing a war but had everything to do with preserving the peace by preserving the past. And it wasn't just a consideration; it was a proclamation from the top man, the commander in chief of Allied forces in Europe.

That proclamation was issued as a memo from Allied Force Headquarters in England on December 29, 1943. It went to "all commanders" in Italy. It was signed by General Dwight D. Eisenhower.

And it said: "Today we are fighting in a country (Italy) which has contributed a great deal to our cultural inheritance, a country rich in monuments which by their creation helped and now in their old age illustrate the growth of the civilization which is ours. We are bound to respect those monuments so far as war allows.

"If we have to choose between destroying a famous building and sacrificing our own men, then our men's lives count infinitely more and the buildings must go. But the choice is not always so clear-cut as that. In many cases the monuments can be spared without any detriment to operational needs. Nothing can stand against the argument of military necessity. That is an accepted principle. But the phrase 'military necessity' is sometimes used where it would be more truthful to speak of military convenience or even of personal convenience. I do not want it to cloak slackness or indifference.

"It is a responsibility of higher commanders to determine... the location of historical monuments whether they be immediately ahead of our front lines or in areas occupied by us.

This information passed to lower echelons through normal channels places the responsibility on all commanders of complying with the spirit of this letter."

So Italy—like Greece a treasure trove of ancient buildings, statues, monuments and works of art—had an official blessing to preserve its past, provided, of course, that the lives of Allied troops and airmen were not put in harm's way. At times, the past was relegated to the trash bin when to do otherwise would have meant sacrificing men. At times, mistakes were made. And, at times perhaps, the plan to preserve historic sites was simply overlooked.

Thanks to such directives from those who led the war effort, much did survive, as proven today by the sights of Rome and Florence and a host of other cities. But Eisenhower's letter went beyond merely avoiding the bombing or shelling of sites that had witnessed the evolution of civilization. It was interpreted by Allied commanders to also protect art treasures from common thievery. There were exceptions, no doubt; there always are. But the vast majority of Allied troops who were fighting through the Continent, and at times collecting souvenirs, avoided the theft of major works of art. Not so the Nazis!

On May 8, 1944, the Mediterranean Allied Tactical Air Force headquarters issued a three-page pamphlet "to outline the history of art in Italy" and to impress on its troops that they had better not paint a black mark on that history, as the Nazis had.

"The Nazis have systematically stripped large parts of Europe of their movable works of art," the pamphlet charged, adding that "Much of the booty has passed into hands of the Party leaders."

The document named names, not as a means of any legal maneuver but simply as a way of impressing its troops with the gravity of the situation. For example, it said that the German foreign minister, Joachim von Ribbentrop, "sent a special convoy of lorries (trucks) to rob the museums of Athens." It noted that Hermann Goering—whose distinguished record as a pilot in World War I was overshadowed by his greed and lack of leadership over Germany's air force in World War II— "has a fine collection of modern French art," while Hitler's propagandist Paul Goebbels "is said to prefer the Flemish painters."

According to the pamphlet, some of the confiscated artwork from Europe was to be sent to the city of Linz in northern Austria "as a memorial to Hitler's mother." And it termed the looting of art treasures across Europe by the Nazis "organized robbery."

The pamphlet went beyond art by stating: "It is the policy of this command to avoid attacking installations of a medical, religious or historical nature whenever possible." It published lists of protected monuments for the benefit of its air crews and it warned all personnel against the defacing of works of art, offering such straight-forward advice as: "don't carve your name."

Avoiding such treasures became another problem for bomber crews.

4 RETURN TO PLOESTI

A relief from daily flights did not last long. Two days after the unsuccessful raid against Ploesti, Fritz's group was airborne again. The target was a railroad bridge used by the Germans to move equipment and supplies in the southeastern corner of France, not far from the Italian border. Officially, the site was at Var but Fritz's pilot described it in more general terms. It was near Nice, he said, and the tiny principality of Monaco.

Two days on the ground had given the crew a chance to talk and rest. They were growing closer by the day. "We were a good crew," Fritz said. "You need to get along to be a good crew, and we got along."

After the Ploesti raid and its heavy flak, despite the fact that they returned safely, there was a sense among the crew that a trip across Italy, out over the Tyrrhenian Sea and above Corsica to the French coast for a hit on a single bridge would be a milk run, which meant light to moderate flak. It was anything but.

The bridge was hit from 21,000 feet but the altitude did not save the American bombers from trouble. Fritz's B-24 lost one of its four engines, and the nose turret was struck hard by flak four times. It limped back to Foggia and landed with a skimpy fifty gallons of gasoline still in the tanks. A count by mechanics found forty-five flak holes in the ship. No one was wounded but it had been a long eight-hour day.

Weather during the next two days kept the bombers at Foggia grounded, but on the third day crews were awakened in the morning darkness and summoned to the briefings. The target again was Ploesti and specifically what had come to be known as the American refinery outside the city. It was one of the large facilities established by other countries long before the war had broken out and then taken over by the Romanians and the Germans. It had been set up by an American oil company as had other refineries in that region by other private firms from around the world. Take out the American refinery? The question was easily answered because airmen knew the pirated plant was now pumping out lifeblood for Hitler's Third Reich.

The flak again was heavy, even at 23,000 feet. But the plant was heavily damaged. On the American side, one B-24 — plane number 44, Fritz recalls — went down over the target. For some reason, apparently never explained, the crews were given only a single-mission credit for the attack even though their run over the refineries less than a week earlier resulted in credit for two missions. And that first raid resulted in no damage because of the dense cover from ground smoke pots.

It was a long stretch between the second Ploesti flight and the next assignment, four whole days. But the destination, much like Ploesti, could strike fear in the hearts of Allied flyers. It was over Austria again, this time to a place called Neubing which Fritz's pilot said was en route to Munich, Germany. Double mission credit would be tallied because Neubing was the site of a major German airfield. They would be going in to damage the runways, destroy planes on the ground (if any) and knock down as much of the infrastructure as possible. The bomb run would be from 24,000 feet.

"We had plenty of escorts going in and coming away from the target," said Fritz. "I only saw a few German fighters in the air. The flak looked heavy but we didn't seem to get into the thick of it," an indication that enemy gunners may not have been setting their fuses to explode at a high-enough altitude.

There was another day of rest for the 376th Bombardment Group and then an attack planned the following day, again in Austria but farther north than Neubing. They would fly to within fifteen miles of the Czechoslovakian border, to a place near the city of Linz called Horshing. It was another Nazi airfield, heavily defended of course. This mission had special significance, not because of the target but because of the location. Linz was the hometown of Adolf Hitler.

"We were supposed to go in at 24,000 feet but the cloud cover was up to 30,000, so we turned around and went home without dropping a bomb," Fritz remembered. "I saw four Messerschmitt 109s (the leading German fighter with more than 30,000 built) but they gave us no trouble."

Three days passed before the next briefing for the group. They would be going to Genoa, Italy, at the opposite end of the country, to the birthplace of Christopher Columbus, to a shipyard in the Ligurian Sea, a northern segment of the Mediterranean. The altitude would be 22,000 and flak would be "moderate," the briefing officer predicted. What neither he nor anyone else could predict was that the lead plane, the one all

This photo of one B-24 taken from another aircraft over Italy shows how closely bombers flew on their missions.
Courtesy of the National Archives and Records Administration

others follow in and imitate, could not get its bomb bay doors open. The target went unscathed.

In World War II bomb runs, when radio silence was in effect, bombardiers in formation did what the bombardier in the lead plane did. When they saw his bombs dropping they released theirs too. If, for whatever reason, his bombs weren't released theirs weren't either.

Unlike their first week in combat, Fritz's crew was now flying about every other day or even every third day. After the dry run to Genoa they were selected for another trip to Markersdorf, Austria, again with double-mission credit for an expected tough ride. They would strike the airfields there again, this time from 19,000 feet, three thousand lower than the first time. They were carrying 240 fragmentation bombs, each weighing twenty pounds, designed to kill or injure enemy troops. But bad weather became a critical factor and the group missed the target. Flak this time was only moderate although Fritz did help fight off five attacking ME-109s.

Four days passed before his group was called again. For the first time, they would be entering Hungarian airspace with a run to Lispe, near Budapest, a round trip estimated at six hours and thirty minutes. The target was a refinery and the bomb run would be at 19,000 feet. There would be no friendly fighter escort going in or coming out.

"We hit the target," Fritz said. "I saw flames and smoke. The flak was quite heavy but, thank goodness, we saw no enemy fighters."

Fortunately, for all Allied airmen, the Luftwaffe was losing its supply of good pilots. There was no rotation system for them, no 35 or 50 missions and home plan. The German airmen, now defending their homeland, flew until they were killed or too badly wounded or captured. Added to that was the growing reduction in oil products, which in 1945 had the Luftwaffe using horses to tow its new jet fighters from the airport aprons to the runways just to save fuel on taxiing. A third problem was the constant Allied hammering of aircraft production facilities and the resulting drop in available fighters to stop the onslaught of American and British bombers.

Three days later, the call was to the famous Brenner Pass, a gateway from Italy into Austria. The target was a railway bridge up past Trento near a town named Avisio.

The B-24s came in at 20,000 feet, swam through heavy flak, hit the bridge and turned for home. "Good cover" from thirty P-38s prevented any problem with fighter planes, but the flak did its dirty work. Seven hours later, on the ground in Foggia, Fritz and his crew examined a large hole in one wing; it measured six inches across.

Another three days passed before the next mission. It was a repeat of Fritz's first raid a month earlier. They would be flying over Rome, crossing the Tyrrhenian Sea, slipping by Corsica and coming into Toulon, France, over the Mediterranean. It was the German submarine pens again, one of the homes used by the marauding U-boats to menace the Med, and it would be tough.

At 23,000 feet, the group bounced through heavy flak but they put their bombs in the right spot. On the way out, Fritz

Four bombs fall from a B-24 nicknamed "Smitty" on a target in Europe.
Courtesy of U.S. Air Force Historical Research Agency, Maxwell AFB

watched a B-24 with the tail number 55 go down in flames. His bomber got back to Foggia with another large hole in a wing.

Fritz now had a total of eighteen missions to his credit, just over halfway to the required thirty-five that won a ticket back to the States. But halfway was also an unlucky position. Most Allied airmen knew that their luck was running out because most never got halfway.

5 · THE FINAL RUN

Four days passed before Fritz's next mission was called. He now had about one hundred hours of combat flying, one hundred hours of boredom en route to a target followed by sheer terror on the run in, the enemy fighters, the flak, the bomb release and the harrowing trips out to safety. The missions took their tolls on all the airmen. The chance their plane would be hit was extremely high, almost a foregone conclusion. The chance they would be wounded was fairly high. The chance they would be shot down—particularly after logging so many missions—was ever present. The chance they would die was not a subject for conversation, nor a reason to run from their responsibility, but ever a thought in the back of every man's mind.

With each mission tucked into his record, the airman did not want to weigh his odds of survival; he wanted to do his job and go home. Fritz, like others, was satisfied that he was performing a function which eventually could help bring peace and stability back to the human race. And, like others, he never thought he was doing anything heroic. He was just performing the way he had been trained to perform, knowing full well that he had shot down some German fighters. That's why he was there.

He didn't mind the living conditions; he knew they were only temporary. The meals on base weren't bad; he had lived through the Depression when things were worse. There was a goodly amount of fresh food available, something he knew a lot of guys pounding across the mud of battlefields didn't have. Years later, he recalled "there was always a lot of stew" in the mess hall. But he liked stew. He was from the hard coal region where life could be difficult and dangerous and not filled with a wide variety of difference from day to day.

On the base everyone tried to improve — as conditions allowed — daily life. And that included cooking food outside the mess hall. The men built stoves, fueled by one hundred octane gasoline which lent a sense of living on the edge, for gasoline could explode as well as burn. But living on the edge had become part of their daily routine, on the ground or in the air. They put flat rocks on the makeshift stoves and fried eggs.

They paid nearby residents to clean their clothes, even providing some of that volatile gasoline for the purpose. In a war economy it was work the local people desired because it gave them money to buy food rather than scrounging through trash cans for scraps. If there was one thing which really bothered the Allied airmen it was seeing the war-weary Italians — the elderly, the young and everyone in between — eating food they picked out of the garbage. It particularly bothered Fritz when he saw civilians even chewing on bare bones for any slight amount of nourishment.

"We got plenty of food on base," he said. But there was a reason. Airmen couldn't fly day-long missions, fighting fatigue, fright and frigid temperatures unless they kept up their strength with a solid diet. And, as much as they wanted to, they could not feed the entire Italian population, even just around Foggia.

At the briefing the next morning, there was a gasp when the target was announced: Ploesti! Again! The eleven oil refineries surrounding the city had been taking a pounding but were still producing the products needed to fuel and lubricate Hitler's war machine. It would be hit and hit again until the flow of those products was stopped. Ploesti had been a city of 100,000 in 1941 but the Germans had evacuated all non-essential people in order to make the refinery circle a virtual fortress against air attacks.

It would be Fritz's nineteenth mission, his third across the Adriatic and Yugoslavia to the far side of Romania. The first two missions to Ploesti had met heavy resistance. He compared them to the other seventeen trips his crew had made, and the answer was always the same: Ploesti is the worst. Some missions had turned out to be the so-called "milk runs," although a civilian today would most assuredly class them as extremely dangerous trips. Even on milk runs bombers returned to base with holes in the wings, tail and fuselage.

It was a clear day when they took off at 7 a.m. The run to target four hours later would be at 22,500 feet. The usual resistance was predicted: enemy fighters going in and coming out; the usual Ploesti intense flak; possibly smoke from the ground pots. They had a passenger on board, a ground crew member of Fritz's squadron who had never flown but who needed a mission like this to get an early ticket home. He was officially classified as a combat photographer. Fritz thought it strange that the guy would pick a Ploesti run to pick up that ticket, or perhaps he didn't have a choice.

The raiders went through it all, dropped their bombs and were turning away from the refineries, turning toward Italy and home base. On Fritz's plane the number one engine went out! Then the number three caught fire! One of the two remaining began acting up too. A pilot could fly a B-24 on two engines, but not very fast, not fast enough to keep up with the safety of the bomber formation. But one engine could not keep the plane aloft.

Then a gas tank took a hit and precious fuel was spewing out behind one wing!

Smoke from explosions caused by other aircraft rises in the background as three B-24s head for their target over the vast Ploesti oil refineries.

Courtesy of the National Air and Space Administration

As smoke from bombing rises beneath them, four B-17s head for another oil refinery in the massive ring around Ploesti.

Courtesy of the National Air and Space Administration

At least seven B-24s are visible as they pass through smoke rising from oil pots set afire by German defenders at Ploesti.

Courtesy of the National Air and Space Administration

After hitting their target at Ploesti, two B-17s leave the area as another group of B-17s (at least seven) fly far below.
Courtesy of the National Air and Space Administration

Bombs fall from a B-24 over Ploesti, Romania.
Courtesy of the National Air and Space Museum

Over the intercom came word that the navigator was seriously wounded. Shrapnel had slammed into his chest. The bombardier and the nose turret gunner, also up front, had been wounded too.

Again, word from the pilot, the aircraft controls were not responding as they should. Shrapnel or enemy fighter bullets had punctured the fuselage and damaged or destroyed the lines which controlled the pilot's ability to turn or bank or climb. Pieces of metal from the supercharger on one engine were flying back and striking the plane's waist.

Then the intercom failed. The engineer moved back through the plane to summon Fritz from his position in the tail, telling him to move forward to the waist and prepare to bail out. Within minutes the decision was changed. The new plan was to head east rather than west. Try to reach Russian territory because they didn't have the power to get home. Try to crash-land in Allied territory even though they weren't sure what kind of treatment they would receive from the Soviets.

Go back to your tail gun, Fritz was told. He could hear guns firing but didn't know by whom. When he got back to his position he found out. The Plexiglas shield around his seat was shot full of holes. If he had been sitting there he would have been full of holes too.

Change of plans again! Fritz was told to move forward again to the waist. The B-24 was now down to six thousand feet and losing altitude rapidly. It was lumbering along. They couldn't make it to Russian territory and they couldn't get home. It was very doubtful that they could even make a successful crash-landing, but crash they would if they didn't get out. The order was given: "Bail out! Bail out!"

The passenger with the camera panicked. This was a ticket home, not a jump into bare sky. He grabbed a hydraulic line which ran along the fuselage when the waist gunner told him to jump and refused. "It took two guys to throw him out," Fritz said, "and I went through the small hatch in the belly," still dressed in his heated flight suit and cloth boots. He had never parachuted before; it was not something they did in training. They learned only how to pull the rip cord, hang on to the straps and hope for a decent landing. But they never went through an actual jump. This one was for real.

The slipstream of the crippled B-24 threw him violently back and down. His mind blanked out momentarily and he forgot all about the rip cord. But once out of that rush of wind Fritz regained control of his mind and body. There was no sensation of falling as he calmly pulled the rip cord. A momentary scene flooded his mind, that of a parachute rigger telling him the old joke about bringing the chute back if it didn't open. It wasn't funny then and it wasn't funny now, he thought. When the parachute blossomed out above him he felt a momentary relief that he would not die in a free fall to the ground. He tried desperately to steer the straps to ensure he would not drift into nearby woods and get hung up or, worse, impaled on a tree. There seemed to be no wind and he concentrated on the drop, telling himself to go limp before hitting the ground.

But just as he thought all was going well, he heard the whizzing by of bullets. In an instant, fear gripped Fritz that he would be shot to death while still in the air. He looked down but could not see anyone shooting. He looked to his front but could see no other parachutes. He couldn't turn to look for parachutes or the falling Liberator behind. He was alone and someone was shooting at him.

The falling airman estimated he was still a hundred feet up when it seemed the ground "was coming up to meet me." He was dropping onto a farm and hit the ground hard next to a cornfield. He hauled in his billowing parachute to avoid detection by whomever had been shooting and buried it in the field. Then he felt his feet and his legs to see if anything had been broken. Luckily, he was in one piece and on the ground. But where was he? It had to be still Romania; there hadn't been time to fly to any border. He could be close to Ploesti; he just didn't know.

Fritz had no idea where his plane was. In the ground by now? Still flying and losing altitude? Still with someone, or several men, still on board?

At first, he heard no sounds. Nothing was above him in the sky. The field was apparently empty, save for him. But he was in the open, out where he could be seen. And where was that mysterious gunman who shot at him? He moved quickly out of the field and into the woods. His bailout kit included a compass and map, but what good would that do? He had no idea of where he was or where he was going, which way was safe and which way led to capture or death.

Then came voices, definitely neither American nor English. Not far away he could see soldiers with a horse and wagon. Some were in what he recognized as German army uniforms; the others, he assumed, must be Romanian troops. They were yelling loudly, obviously looking for him or others who had parachuted out of the stricken B-24. "Comrade, comrade, comrade" was the only word he recognized. Fritz stayed down, hopefully out of sight. The soldiers moved on, their voices trailing off in the distance.

In the nearby woods, he could see two people moving about slowly. He recognized their uniforms and then their faces. They were his copilot and the waist gunner. He called out their names, almost in a whisper. The two turned and smiled. Did others get out? Fritz asked. The copilot confirmed that everyone had jumped but he had no idea where they had landed or whether they were safe.

In training, air crews had been told to move only at night to avoid being spotted and captured. But, Fritz recalled, the waist gunner convinced the copilot they should hide in the woods all night and move the next morning. It was the wrong move.

The three men were free for some eighteen hours, including a damp night in the woods where they lay huddled together for warmth. Early the next day they were surprised by four Romanian peasants threatening them with pitchforks. Fritz recalled the stories he had heard of downed airmen being executed by civilians enraged by the bombing of their homes or place of employment or just their locality. Facing pitchforks and a language barrier, none of the three Americans knew what was being said or planned by the Romanians. But the longer they were held captive the more convinced they were that these country folk meant them no personal harm. The three were loaded into a farm wagon, still under guard, and sat for hours as horses pulled the wagon over rutted dirt roads. "I wanted to jump from the wagon, but I'm glad I didn't," Fritz said. "They would have killed me."

After traveling nearly all day, they approached a city which turned out to be Bucharest, thirty-five miles south of Ploesti, where they were turned over to German troops for hours of interrogation. It was then they fully realized they were now officially prisoners of war. The first thing that surprised Fritz was that the German interrogators already knew much about the captured airmen, including their unit and the location of their base.

Fritz's experiences parallel reports released years after the war by the 15th Air Force which show that, generally, Romanian civilians were friendly to downed airmen. And it wasn't unusual for the airmen to be captured by pitchfork-armed Romanians in the countryside, but no violence ever occurred. In fact, many American fliers were first taken to a farm house and fed while the local police were contacted. However, the Romanian people remained loyal to their country and turned over captured airmen as soon as possible.

In the custody of Romanian police or soldiers, airmen said they were well treated. Many said they were questioned about their aircraft and their target, but since the questions were not of a technical nature they felt the asking came more from curiosity than a military need-to-know. One navigator who was dealing with top-secret equipment in his bomber was asked why the plane was carrying two navigators. He replied simply that he was keeping an eye on the second man; no further questions were asked.

Most men shot down near Ploesti were questioned briefly at army headquarters in that city before being transported to Bucharest. Then many were first taken to King Michael's Regiment Garrison for further questioning and given a form containing personal questions. Their answers, they were told, were necessary for notifying the International Red Cross of their location. Most said they answered the personal questions but all said they refused to answer any questions of a military nature. A few men were put into solitary confinement for forty-eight hours for refusing to answer any questions. One Jewish airman said the Romanian authorities threatened to turn him over to the Germans if he refused to answer questions. He still refused, but the threat was not carried out.

6 ⟩ A PRISONER OF WAR

As was standard procedure in wartime, the captured enlisted men and officers were placed in different sections of a prisoner-of-war camp run by the Germans and guarded by the Romanians. But it took little time for Fritz to learn that every officer and enlisted member of his crew had survived and that all were prisoners. Even the navigator, carrying a chest full of shrapnel, made it safely to the ground, as did the wounded bombardier and nose turret gunner. So did their passenger, the photographer, though he broke a leg on the jump.

Three days later, Fritz's parents received the terrible news that their son was missing. The telegram from Washington said: "The Secretary of War desires me to express his deep regret that your son, Staff Sergeant Harry B. Fritz, has been reported missing in action over Romania. If further details or other information are received you will be promptly notified." That could mean dead, dying, wounded, on the run or captured. His parents didn't know.

The prisoners were housed in old buildings on what seemed to be the outskirts of Bucharest. Barbed wire fences separated the officers and enlisted men, and other fences kept them from the city streets. It was the beginning of a period of

WESTERN UNION

A. N. WILLIAMS
PRESIDENT

The filing time shown in the date line on telegrams and day letters is STANDARD TIME at point of origin. Time of receipt is STANDARD TIME at point of destination

Mrs Lillian I.Fritz
249 South Main St
Pine Grove,Pa.
         The Secretary of War desires me to express his deep regret that
your son Staff Sergeant Harry B.Fritz has been reported missing in action
over Rumania .If futher details or other information
are received you will be promptly notified.

                    J.A.ULIO The Adjutant General.

First of three telegrams received by the parents of Staff Sergeant Harry Fritz reports him missing in action.

Harry Fritz Collection

hunger, thirst, sickness and uncertainty. Would they be shipped to a stalag in Germany? Would they end up in the hands of the German air force, which rumor said would mean better treatment than a camp run by the Gestapo? Would they be exposed to the wrath of civilians who may have been the victims of their bomb runs? There were no answers!

His first night in a prison camp was memorable — a bed of thin straw on a concrete floor. Later, each man got a bunk, but still had only the straw for comfort. At least they thought the straw would be comfortable, until they found it was crawling with lice. From then on, spare time was spent sitting outside picking lice off their clothing, out of their hair and off their bodies.

Their diet, he learned early, would be bread, broth, a kind of tea which some men thought looked like hydraulic fluid, and water. Day in, day out, the same food appeared. It was cooked by prisoners. The unwrapped bread was stacked on a wagon, exposing it to flies and other insects before it got to the prisoners. In time, everyone began to lose weight, suffer from the effects of a bad diet, and wonder when — or if — their ordeal would end.

There were also a few British prisoners in Fritz's camp and, in a neighboring camp, Russians.

The routine never changed. Each day, every man was herded single file through what looked like a cattle chute and counted. Fritz recalled that one day an American prisoner thumbed his nose at the guards. "He was taken away; we never saw him again."

Prisoners learned to keep their mouths shut and to behave. Those who didn't, like the nose thumber, were taken away, never to return to the camp. Those who followed the rules were not abused, Fritz said. There was nothing to gain and everything to lose by not following the rules. Despite postwar stories and Hollywood films about escapes or attempts to escape, most POWs never tried. It wasn't because they didn't want to. Rather, it was because remaining prisoners might be punished if someone ran off. And, if caught, escapees could face execution. In addition, most prisoners had little idea where they were or, if they did know, realized they were so far from Allied lines that escape would be almost impossible. Many were too sick or weak to get very far anyway. Most spoke none of the local languages and did not know whom they could trust if they did get beyond a stockade fence. Escape was not a good option; survival was the key.

In reports declassified years after the war and released by the U.S. Air Force, former prisoners told 15th Air Force investigators that they had not been subjected to particularly bad treatment, although the food was quite poor. They said Romanian guards were friendly to them but were too frightened of their own officers to assist the Americans. Romanian interrogating officers visited the camps frequently and appeared friendly.

It was also generally understood that living conditions in the enlisted men's camps were not as good as those in the officers' camps, particularly when it came to food. The enlisted men said they apparently got the same rations as the

Romanian soldiers, which consisted of a vegetable soup as the staple meal of the day. They also received a cup of weak tea or coffee and a piece of black bread for breakfast.

There was little to do in the camps, although some men tried to play volleyball. Some POWs said later that a woman from the Romanian Blue Cross tried to supply the prisoners with books. Religious services were held on Sundays in the officers' camps, and later, when the officers demanded it, a chaplain was allowed to conduct services in the enlisted men's camps.

Washing facilities in all camps were poor, although there seemed to be a sufficient supply of cold water. The only latrines available were those in which the men were forced to squat above holes in the floors; there were never enough to accommodate the number of prisoners.

The airmen told the 15th Air Force investigators that in the area of medical treatment their biggest problem "seemed to be the absolute lack of interest the Romanian authorities had in either their own or the American sick." For example, dressings for wounds were left on for extremely long periods without being changed, although it appeared there was no shortage of medical supplies. One investigator who reported his findings in writing made this notation: "At least one American airman's death can be put down to lack of interest and another to carelessness." Until June 1944, the only POW hospital in Bucharest was being run by one American officer and three sergeants who had to make the beds, wash the patients, clean the wards and do all the other nursing work. The only time they saw nurses, the investigator reported, was when the Romanian medical officer made his rounds about twice a week.

Another air force investigative report said that "one POW with seven (wounds) had his arm and part of his body in a plaster cast with access to only one wound. Naturally, the remainder went bad so that he contracted lockjaw. He was taken away and cured of that but died a few days after his return, with no attempt being made to remove the plaster cast. Another patient during the amputation of his leg...was having fluid pumped into his system. Through carelessness, air was allowed in so that the patient began to swell at all the weak points of his arteries and died shortly afterwards."

The hospital — really just four small rooms — housed thirty enlisted men and ten officers. They slept on bed boards laid on the floors and covered with thin straw mattresses. The single sheet which covered each man was changed about once a month. Although water was plentiful in the hospital no soap was provided. A collection was taken up in the main camp so that soap could be purchased in the city. Towels were not available. The facility had only two squat-type latrines for the forty-one patients and one of them was generally not operational.

The hospital had no electric lights, although in the summer months that was generally considered not a hardship during the long days. Because of the overcrowding and the odors from neglected wounds, the smell in the four rooms was "unbearable." Food for the patients had to be carried from the main camp and consisted of the same diet that all prisoners faced: a weak vegetable soup for lunch and dinner, weak tea or coffee, and a piece of bread for breakfast. Although milk was sometimes issued in the hospital there were no special diets for prisoners suffering from jaundice, ulcers or stomach problems. Before May 1944, no Red Cross packages were received although patients were visited frequently by the woman from the Romanian Blue Cross, who provided the only books available to the men.

The hospital had no operating room or areas for dressing wounds. Men who required special treatment or operations were carried by stretcher through the city streets to another hospital three-quarters of a mile away. Immediately after the treatment or operation, they were carried back to the POW ward.

Occasionally, sulfa drugs — which probably came from captured American airmen's escape kits — were used, but their effectiveness was dimmed by the length of time wounds were left without the dressings being changed, sometimes as long as fifteen days. Iodine seemed to be in plentiful supply and was used for multiple disinfecting jobs.

In June 1944, the patients were moved to a new two-story building still under construction. The Americans were given half of the second floor while Romanians with venereal diseases were housed in the other half. The POWs now had regular spring hospital beds, but still only got one sheet per bed which had to be washed frequently by the three sergeants until the monthly change of sheets. A Romanian nurse volunteered to help the sergeants with their daily work, which meant that treatment improved and dressings were changed more often. This building did not have treatment or operating rooms either, so stretcher carrying through the streets continued. Only one sink was available for all of the POW patients and they had to share filthy latrine facilities with the Romanian venereal disease patients.

Someone suggested the men in Fritz's camp do something creative to keep their minds off their predicament. So they did; they wrote a song. It was the story of their situation. It didn't take their minds off the predicament; in fact, that's what the song was all about. But at least it relieved some of the boredom. They called it the "Bucharest Cannonball" and it went like this:

Across the Adriatic, through spacious skies of blue,
There came a thousand bombers, with airmen tried and true.
They headed through the Balkans and straight for
    Bucharest,
But when they reached Flak Alley the gunners did the rest.
They all landed safely, with parachutes galore,
And now we're in a prison camp, a-sweating out the war.
A train pulled into Bucharest one warm and sunny day.
As we went through the city, we heard the people say,
"You're murderers, you're gangsters, you've bombed
    our city fair.

You've just knocked out our marshalling yards,
Which are now beyond repair."
But, we all landed safely, with parachutes galore
And now we're in a prison camp, a-sweating out the war.
You may think that ends our story, with nothing else a-do.
We thought the war was over, but the bombers they
        still flew;
We heard the roar of engines as they passed overhead;
We heard the bombs a-whistling and dived beneath our bed.
We lay there a-tremblin' and praying very hard,
That they would miss the city and hit the marshalling yard.

Harry Fritz can sing that song to this day. And, according to one 1945 news account, there are other verses which "can't go into a family newspaper." The story went on to say that "the tune was a straight steal from 'The Wabash Cannonball,' but from there on all similarity ends."

The only sign of home (at least home on the base in Italy) was from the sightings of American bombers flying high

Allied POWs in a variety of uniforms pose for the camera. Note the bombed-out buildings in the background.

Harry Fritz Collection

Allied prisoners at Bucharest line up in a bomb crater created by a German aerial attack on the camp after Romania switched sides from the Axis to the Allies. This and other photographs from the prison camp were believed taken by a Romanian guard.

Harry Fritz Collection

Forcing smiles are four prisoners in the Bucharest camp.

Harry Fritz Collection

Two men dig in a bomb crater at the prison camp as other prisoners watch.
Harry Fritz Collection

Prisoners pose in front of a building with shattered windows, the result of an attack by German fighter planes. The man standing in line at the far left is believed to be a Romanian army guard.

Harry Fritz Collection

overhead on continuing raids to Ploesti and other targets. Some were even bombing the railroad marshalling yards which surrounded Bucharest and were within sight of the camp.

The pounding had gone on all summer. In July, Ploesti had been hit so hard that production was limited. On August 3, the 15th Air Force sent four hundred bombers to attack four aircraft factories in southern Germany and railway lines in the Brenner Pass to cut German routes into Italy. Four days later, the 15th sent 365 planes to hit synthetic oil plants in Silesia and within forty-eight hours struck refineries, oil storage depots and airbases in Hungary with 250 aircraft. Meanwhile, the assault continued against Ploesti too where five—almost half—of the refineries were heavily damaged.

In the days and weeks to come, Fritz and his compatriots began to feel the physical effects of prison camp life. He, like many others, came down with dysentery—that wretched abdominal pain with spasms, passing blood and mucus. Everyone assumed it came from bad drinking water and bad food, but there was neither solution nor cure for the men. It doubled them over and disabled them. It made life even more unbearable. In time, due to dysentery and a host of other medical problems, prisoners began to lose weight.

One of the other men captured that summer was a twenty-eight-year-old pilot from Dallas, Texas, who survived a mid-air explosion over Ploesti which blew him out of his B-24 and killed the rest of his crew. Lt. Col. William G. Snaith, in the army since 1934, had completed forty-one combat missions and was commanding the 4th Wing from the 15th Air Force when his Liberator exploded. In a statement later, he told interrogators that he felt the plane lurch, apparently hit by flak after the bomb run over one of the major refineries. He looked around, saw the bomb bays in a mass of flames and was knocked unconscious as the plane blew up. When Snaith came to he was falling through the sky but had enough presence of mind to pull his rip cord.

Landing in low ground near the target area, he felt the blasts of bombs from other planes and was covered in dust from the explosions. His freedom lasted some four hours before German and Romanian troops captured him. From those soldiers and later from other prisoners he learned the awful truth that no one else in his crew had survived.

A German medic treated second-degree burns on Snaith's face before guards took him to a hospital. The next day he was transferred to a camouflaged prisoner-of-war camp at Ploesti. Under interrogation by the Germans, Snaith refused to answer questions about his mission. Later that day, he was taken to another camp in Bucharest and questioned by Romanian military authorities. Again, he refused to answer questions. Two of the questions he was asked in both camps concerned the attitude of the United States toward Russia and why the United States "was fighting England's war." One of the questioners told him that the Russians would ruin "continental culture." Snaith refused to respond.

There were a number of POW camps in that part of Romania but as the local situation changed, men were moved. Of those shot down in the Ploesti low-level raid of August 1, 1943, thirty-nine officers and seventy-one enlisted men had been kept in a camp at Tinisul de Jos, about seven miles south of the city of Brasov and seventy-five miles north of Bucharest, but the wounded from that group were moved fifteen miles further south to a military hospital. Other American airmen were housed in the military garrison next to a sports stadium in Bucharest until May 8 when they were sent to two camps, the enlisted men to a military hospital near the north train station in the city and the officers to southcentral Bucharest. On August 23, both groups were transported to an army garrison five miles southwest of the city.

In late August, word spread throughout Fritz's camp that a Soviet army was approaching Romania. The Germans abandoned the camp, moving most of their troops further north, up toward Ploesti, to avoid the dreaded Russians. Fighting between the German and Soviet armies on the Eastern Front had left bitter memories. Neither side had any compassion whatsoever for the other. When the Germans pulled out they left only Romanian troops to guard the prisoners. But there was one satisfying element of the pullout: the Germans did not try to move the Allied prisoners north with them, as had been rumored they would.

However, for the 110 men of the 1943 raid kept in the Brasov area, the German pullback provided what was later termed a "a harrowing experience." With the help of Romanians opposed to the Nazis, the airmen were to be moved by truck at night to the small city of Pietro Sita. The plan included the storing of guns and ammunition near their camp so that, if German resistance came, the American airmen would fight rather than face a forced march to a POW camp in Germany. As the trucks rolled out of the camp southward they encountered German troops retreating to the north. The prisoner-laden convoy pulled off the road in the darkness and waited for the enemy to pass. The Germans rolled on by, apparently unaware that the covered trucks were taking escaping prisoners to a safer location.

At 11:30 that night, the trucks rolled into Pietro Sita and deposited the airmen—one or two at a time—at the homes of friendly residents of that city.

It has been claimed that one of the people responsible for convincing the Germans not to take the Allied prisoners with them in retreat was a member of Romanian royalty. Her name was Princess Catherine Caradja, called by some "The Angel of Ploesti." But that story, if true, was not her real claim to fame. Princess Catherine, in her early 50s in 1944, is also credited with assisting many downed airmen in the Ploesti-Bucharest area. Some of the American fliers said later that this powerful Romanian woman did more for their morale than anyone or anything else. She visited prison camps in the Bucharest area weekly, provided food and even got them shoes when it was supposedly impossible to obtain them from other sources.

It is known that Princess Catherine had an American who was killed in the crash of his plane buried on her estate. According to a story in the *Kentucky Post* in 1997, Princess Catherine operated an orphanage on that estate after the war, which the postwar Communist governor took away from her in 1952. She told the family of the American whom she had buried that she escaped from Romania after confiscation of her property by hiding in a sealed railroad car until the train got to France. The newspaper said she moved to the United States in 1956, settled in Kansas City and became a guest at several reunions of former Romanian POWs.

Life changed somewhat in the camps after the German guards left. There was a feeling that the Romanian guards were less threatening to the prisoners. But the questions remained: Would the Romanians continue to treat them better? What would happen if the Russians came in? There was no love lost between the Russians and the Romanians. Would the American and British airmen get caught in the middle of a battle? Would the Russians send the prisoners eastward into the Soviet Union where a huge question mark still loomed over what happened to Allied prisoners who disappeared into the vastness of that conglomeration of communist countries. The status quo of the airmen was not good; the future could be even worse.

It didn't take long for the Romanians to see the proverbial handwriting on the wall. With mining of the Danube River and the destruction of roads and rail tracks, the country was becoming isolated from Germany. By late August, the refineries at the huge Ploesti complex were either heavily damaged or completely knocked out. But the scariest part, perhaps, was knowledge that the Soviets were coming. Soviet military strength and numbers were massive. Soviet troops, egged on by Communist Party officers, could be ruthless. Russians, and perhaps all Soviets, did not like the Romanians. And the Soviets were allied with the Americans and British. The consensus in Romania: time to drop the Germans as comrades and join the winning side.

The word came at night on August 23. Romanian guards circulated throughout the officers' and enlisted men's camps and, with flashlights in hand, read in English an official proclamation saying that the prisoners were free.

As soon as the Romanian government announced the switch, its soldiers abandoned the prisoner-of-war camp too. The airmen were free, but free to do what? They were hundreds of miles from any Allied troops. They were still in enemy territory with at least one German airbase a scant twenty miles to the north, some German troops near Bucharest and a Russian army bearing down from the east.

Along with other officers, Lieutenant Colonel Snaith moved out of Bucharest to avoid German bombing, obtained civilian

clothing and bought food. He would report later that a Palestinian named Chanini, who was connected with the British
Royal Air Force, provided him and other Americans with clothing and money to buy food. He also credited a Bucharest family named Bracadihu for helping him find sources of food and
a Jewish man named Shapeiro, living in the city, who hid a
number of prisoners.

Snaith returned to the camp on August 25 to become the
senior officer in command.

By the time German guards abandoned his camp, Fritz
and others were doubled over with dysentery. The morning
after the announcement of Romania's switch to the Allied side,
some of the prisoners wandered into Bucharest to seek assistance. There was none. The civilian population had its own
disastrous situation with lack of food and good water, little
medical attention, and fear of the military, be they airmen flying overhead, or Germans retreating, or Soviets advancing, or
their own troops wondering what to do next. It was a story
repeated around the world that year as civilians bled and died,
or got sicker, or hungrier, or more worried, or more confused.

Fritz couldn't go into the city. Like many others, he was
too sick to move and almost too ill to care what happened. "I
was at the breaking point," he said. "Someone told me to eat a
small square of bread. I had a whole loaf. The guy said to just
keep eating the bread to control the dysentery." The prisoners
who had gone into Bucharest returned to camp, discouraged
that they could get no help.

The Romanian government's switch to the Allied side in-
furiated Hitler. He ordered the Luftwaffe to bomb the capital.
But no one in Berlin could contact Alfred Gerstenberg, the
German commander of the Bucharest area, to schedule the
bombing. What the Nazis in Berlin did not know was that a
Romanian partisan group had nabbed Gerstenberg and his staff
and were holding them for the Russians. Unfortunately, for
both the Allied prisoners and the residents of Bucharest,

Luftwaffe officers at air bases northeast of Ploesti had also picked up the radio orders from Berlin and sent some thirty bombers and dive bombers to inflict damage on the now almost undefended city. The raids began on August 24 and went on almost continuously for 72 hours. Some Romanian troops manning light guns tried to resist but their efforts were in vain.

However, the bombing had a positive effect for the nation as a whole. Outraged by the attacks, the country did more than just turn away from the Germans as an ally; they took them on as an enemy. King Michael declared war; Romanian pilots fought the Luftwaffe in the skies over Bucharest; soldiers captured heavy German flak guns and fired at German planes. And the new Romanian government tried to ensure the safety of the captured airmen, to protect them from German air raids and from the occasional German ground troops who moved through the area on their way north.

When the German planes came, the prisoners scattered. Some fled into what they considered to be the safety of the city. But they found the residents of Bucharest were fleeing also to escape German bombs and strafing. There seemed to be no safe place.

Fritz tried to get away from the prison barracks. Someone told him to go into a fourteen-story concrete building near the camp. He recalled two things about that building: it appeared to have no glass in the windows (perhaps bombed or shot out earlier); it was filled with civilians running back and forth, screaming and yelling about the bombs falling around them, even standing in the window openings to watch the mayhem. Some were probably city residents, but many others, judging from the rags they wore, looked like peasants from the surrounding countryside. From what he could see, he was the only Allied prisoner in the room. He sat in a corner, his legs hunched up and his head between his knees. His insides ached from dysentery. He tried to shut out the noises — the shouting, the screaming, the explosions. But it went on and on. He prayed to God for help, for release from his pain in any way possible. And he wished that another prisoner were there so that he didn't feel so frightfully alone. It was a moment—just like the sight of his tailgun position all shot up, like his parachute jump with someone shooting at him, like his capture by menacing civilians with pitchforks—when he truly felt he might die. "I was ready to break physically and emotionally," he says now. He did the only thing he could: he cried.

The German bombers smothered their former prison camp and then went after the nearby hospital. Prisoners carried wounded and sick military and civilian alike from the building through the streets to find safe places. German planes screamed overhead as the evacuation continued, and one American said later that he felt like his nerves were going to pieces.

When the explosions stopped and the piercing roar of low-flying aircraft stopped, Fritz straightened up, slowly rose to his feet, listened carefully and wandered to the door. The skies were clear. People were moving about, examining craters formed by German bombs and the pockmarks of bullets in the building. He helped, as much as his battered condition allowed, to get those unable to move into a safer place. Then he staggered back through the open gate of the camp. Ahead of him lay the body of an American airman obviously caught outside when the German fighters strafed the open yard. The man was wearing boots, which Harry removed. He had bailed out of his B-24 in the soft, heated "slippers," as he called them, that the crewmen wore to keep warm, leaving his own boots behind. With his new solid footware, he walked slowly into the basement of a two-story building in the camp and sat down in its darkened coolness. He had survived again but wondered now if he would get another chance at life.

That chance came faster than Fritz or anyone imprisoned there could imagine.

7 OPERATION GUNN

Within two days after the German air attacks, the "low-level" raid prisoners of 1943—who had been interned seventy-five miles north of Bucharest and later in the city of Pietro Sita—arrived in Bucharest. Also abandoned by the Germans, they were now in the second year of captivity in Romania. Like others released from prison camps but unable to escape the country they were looking for food, for medical supplies and for help. What they found in the capital was devastation. There were wounded Americans everywhere, without medical care, without enough food, and without hope. Five POWs had died in the German bombing of the city. Four more perished when a stray German cut them down with a machine gun as they tried to get food in a restaurant. Some had been wounded in the air attacks, but many more were still hurting from wounds suffered when they were shot down and captured.

The prisoners, following the lead of one officer, cleaned up the bombed-out hospital and cared for those no longer able to care for themselves. They begged money to buy food, much of it from the Palestinian agent whom British intelligence had parachuted into Romania. The agent had been carrying a large sum of money to buy what he needed in the ongoing effort to push the Germans out of Romania. The first meal bought with those funds gave the POWs a meal they would not forget — roast beef, gravy, potatoes, coffee, cake and beer — a lot of beer.

But everyone knew they couldn't stay. Neither the money nor the food would last, and they couldn't buy the medical attention so badly needed.

An American in the officers' camp decided that drastic action was needed before 1,100 Allied airmen were wounded or killed in future attacks by the enemy, or starved to death, or perished from disease.

"Why not have the 15th Air Force fly us out?" asked Lieutenant Colonel James A. Gunn III, who had piloted one of the Liberators shot down in a Ploesti raid a week earlier. Other prisoners were skeptical but were willing to help formulate any plan that spelled freedom.

Gunn was a thirty-two-year-old from Kelseyville, California, who had joined the Army Air Corps in 1939. He was a wing leader on his thirty-second mission when his bomber was hit by flak. The B-24 was fifteen miles southeast of Ploesti when the order came to bail out. Gunn landed hard in an open field and saw people running toward him. He limped into a cornfield, heard more voices ahead, continued into an adjoining field and tried to hide behind a sheaf of harvested wheat. He could tell from the voices that a large number of people were searching and it didn't take them long to find him. He estimated that seventy-five civilians were with the two armed Romanian soldiers who took him into custody. None were hostile. In fact, Gunn said later that they all appeared friendly and curious.

The crowd accompanied the soldiers who took Gunn to the village of Cornurile and a local military headquarters. Gunn said the crowd seemed to number about three hundred, but still friendly, still curious. Soldiers took all of his possessions, except a cigarette lighter, watch and ring, and gave him a receipt for the items they kept. In the next hour, he was fed and given a place to lie down. Then he was loaded onto a hay cart and moved to a railroad station a half mile from the village.

During a ninety-minute wait at the station, Gunn was given food and cigarettes by civilians. Finally, his guards, tired of waiting for the train, flagged down a car and asked for a lift. The driver took them to another small village about seven miles from Ploesti where German troops observed Gunn but made no attempt to take him from the Romanian guards. Hitchhiking again, the group got another ride to Ploesti where Gunn was taken to army headquarters for questioning. There he saw his bombardier and navigator and, later, five other members of his crew.

Gunn was first interned in a filthy, insect-ridden hut across the road from army headquarters. But it wasn't a safe place. At 9:30 that night, air raid sirens resulted in the new prisoners being loaded on a truck and driven some three miles out of town. They were kept on the truck and surrounded by Romanian soldiers. Gunn learned later that it was an RAF night raid on the refineries. At 10 a.m. the next day, the sirens sounded again and the prisoners were trucked out of town for two hours during an American raid. Such raids continued, one that night and another the following morning. The following day, Gunn, his crew and a few other recently captured Americans were loaded onto a truck for the trip to Bucharest and a permanent camp.

A day after his arrival in Bucharest, Gunn was put into the officers' camp, from where he could see the POW hospital and the enlisted men's camp. As the new senior officer there, he was told by other prisoners that an escape plan was in progress with the building of a tunnel. The following night, August 23, Gunn was one of the first to learn that the Romanian government had decided to abandon the Germans and join the Allies.

The officers asked the camp commandant to provide them with guns to resist any possible German attack on the prison, a request the commandant turned down without having permission, he said, from higher authorities. Later that night, however, the number of Romanian soldiers guarding the camp was tripled and patrols were sent out into the streets of Bucharest to prevent any surprise attack. When firing was heard in the neighborhood, the commandant gave the prisoners a small number of pistols and rifles.

Nothing else happened that night. The next morning, Gunn contacted the enlisted camp and was told that the situation there was well in hand. But within hours, the Germans hit. They came by air to punish Bucharest and the Romanians for their government's decision to switch sides. The gates of both camps were opened and the prisoners allowed to jump into slit trenches for protection. Although bombs fell near the camps there were no casualties among the prisoners. But continuing attacks made the prisoners nervous because they assumed the Germans were targeting them too. Many wanted to leave even though they knew that some German forces still surrounded parts of Bucharest. Some did go, wandering into the city for shelter, for food, for medical supplies, for any help they could get. But fighting inside the city had intensified too. There was, they soon found, no safe place.

One of the officers who walked into the city was looking for a wireless radio to contact 15th Air Force headquarters in Italy. And Colonel Snaith set off to contact the International Red Cross to discuss a possible rescue attempt. The next day, August 25, the Germans began bombing the prison camps themselves, killing one American enlisted man.

"I started asking for someone to see, and finally was taken to the new government to see the minister of war," Gunn said later. "I asked to be allowed to fly to Italy to make known our situation. The minister agreed to help me."

Gunn received permission to radio 15th Air Force headquarters. He filled in the top brass in Bari on the situation but couldn't get into details due to the possibility the Germans would intercept his message. Gunn was told to return to Italy to discuss what had to be done. But how? First, the Romanians loaned him a pilot, a crew and a "beaten-up," old Savoia Maccheti, a tri-motor bomber, for the trip. That flight started at 1 p.m. on August 26 but lasted only a half hour when the plane developed engine trouble and was forced back to Bucharest. When they landed, a Romanian, identified as one of the country's top fighter pilots, was waiting to meet Gunn.

Captain Constantine Cantacuzene just days earlier had been attacking American and British bombers. Now, with his country, he had switched sides. Cantacuzene offered the use of his German ME-109, the plane he had been flying as part of the Axis air forces.

Cantacuzene was described as a handsome, dashing Romanian who had served as chief pilot of the Romanian State Air Lines from 1930 to 1940. At the time he also held a reserve commission in the Romanian Air Force and occasionally demonstrated aerial acrobatics at air shows. When Romania entered the war on the side of Germany, Cantacuzene became commander of the 9th Pursuit Group. In 1944, the 9th was outfitted with German Messerschmitt 109Gs and stationed that August at Roman Airfield 175 miles north of Bucharest. By that summer, Cantacuzene had been credited with sixty-four aerial victories. The Romanians credited pilots with one victory for each engine of downed enemy planes (one victory for single-engine fighters, four victories for a four-engine bomber). His victories included American P-38s, B-24s and B-17s.

On August 23, when the Romanian government switched sides, Cantacuzene was watching the situation very closely. The next night, in a daring maneuver, he led his 9th Group out of German control at Roman Airport and flew to Popesti Airdrome outside Bucharest. Over the next several days, as German bombers punished their former allies and American prisoners, the 9th Pursuit Group shot down twelve German planes, including four knocked out of the skies by Cantacuzene himself. The sudden switch didn't bother the veteran pilot one bit. He was, he said, a soldier who fought whomever he was told to fight.

When Cantacuzene offered Gunn his ME-109 to return to Italy, there was one major problem. Gunn, a bomber pilot, didn't know how to fly it. In addition, the controls were all labeled in German. So, Cantacuzene, the swashbuckling Romanian flier, offered to be the pilot. But how to get a German fighter plane with a Romanian—though English-speaking—pilot to an American military base to summon help?

First, Gunn arranged to have the enemy markings on the plane painted out and American stars painted on. That might help prevent having the plane shot down before it got close to Allied ground. But even if the pilot got to an American base, how does he explain the predicament? Why would anyone believe a Romanian who just days earlier had been an enemy?

There were so many problems but only one answer: Gunn would go too. Even that posed a problem, a major one: the

Former enemies American Lt. Col. James A. Gunn III, *at left*, and Romanian Air Force Capt. Constantine Cantacuzene toast their successful flight to Italy to initiate the rescue of 1,100 Allied airmen from a POW camp at Bucharest. Gunn was doubled up in the radio compartment of Cantacuzene's German fighter plane.
Courtesy of U.S. Air Force Historical Research Agency, Maxwell AFB

U.S. officers in Italy demonstrate the tight space in a German fighter plane occupied by an American pilot who was flown out of Bucharest by a Romanian pilot to begin Operation Reunion.

Courtesy of U.S. Air Force Historical Research Agency, Maxwell AFB

American servicemen examine the German Messerschmitt 109G flown into their Italian base to launch Operation Reunion. The Nazi swastikas were painted out and American flags and stars were painted on to avoid having the aircraft shot down. A Romanian fighter ace piloted the plane from Bucharest with an American pilot riding in a cramped space behind the bottom right side of the flag.

Courtesy of U.S. Air Force Historical Research Agency, Maxwell AFB

109 was a one-seater fighter. "We took the radio out of the fuselage, and I crawled into a hole which was covered by a plate and screwed on, " Gunn said. With help, he squeezed into the hole, pulled up his legs and placed his head between his knees. Would Gunn be able to sit like that for two hours during a flight which he decided had to be made to the 15th Air Force in Italy? There was no choice; he had to go.

There were several other downsides. Gunn would not be able to see where the plane was going and therefore could not help navigate. Flying high might mean a better chance of crossing the Adriatic before being spotted by Allied air defenses. But if they climbed too high, Gunn would either freeze to death in the unheated compartment or suffocate because no oxygen was available there. And, of course, in a war zone an unidentifed aircraft or even a German plane with strange markings would be a target for anti-aircraft guns or Allied fighters.

Gunn could have been signing his own death warrant with this plan to get help. It looked like the chances for success were much slimmer than those for failure.

Maps were produced showing the route and the location of the 15th's major airfield at San Giovanni. It would be a long ride but both men were willing to give it a shot. At 5:20 p.m. on August 27, the German plane with American markings, a Romanian at the controls, and an ex-prisoner stuffed into the fuselage, took off from Bucharest.

Gunn was literally in the dark the whole way. He had no way of knowing if they were flying in the right direction, when they were over the Adriatic, or how close they were to San Giovanni until he heard and felt the wheels being lowered two hours later. After the 109 touched down and rolled out it was surrounded by a lot of people with a lot of guns. The Romanian stood up in the cockpit, told the Americans he had a surprise for them, asked for a screwdriver, and went right to the radio compartment. When it was opened, a booted foot popped out, then another, then legs, then a whole man

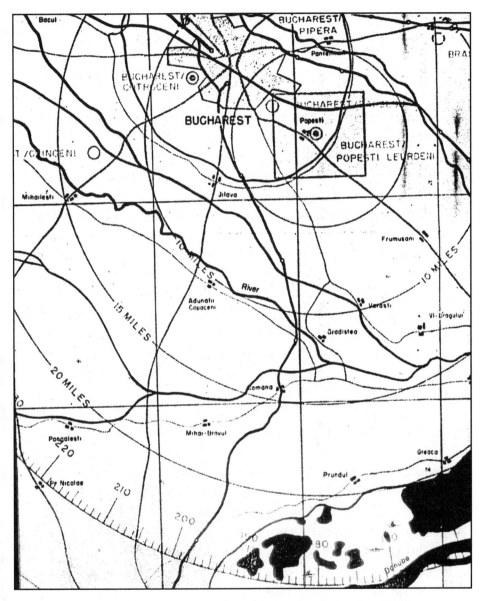

This portion of a World War II navigator's aerial chart shows the city of Bucharest at top center and Popesti, site of a Romanian airfield, to the southeast. B-17s from the 15th Air Force landed at Popesti in 1944 to rescue some 1,100 Allied airmen from a nearby prison camp.

who was immediately recognized by at least one airman in the welcoming committee as Colonel Gunn.

"It wasn't a pleasant trip," Gunn said.

Part One of the mission had been accomplished. Part Two was undertaken immediately. Gunn was flown to nearby Bari to fill in Brigadier General Charles Born, director of operations for the 15th Air Force, on the situation in Bucharest: 1,100 airmen free but with nowhere to run, little food, no medicine, under threat of attack. Something had to be done and done quickly.

First, they agreed a mission was needed to take out the aircraft and airfields from which the Germans had hurled their attacks on the prison camp. Then a rescue operation had to be launched. The planning went on through the next day.

Wing commanders were summoned quickly to Bari to be briefed on Gunn's dramatic flight in the German plane and his announcement that Popesti Airdrome on the outskirts of Bucharest was firmly held by Romanian forces. Then they were told that the 15th Air Force would conduct two operations to rescue the Allied airmen.

The first field order said: "This Air Force will execute an operation to be known as Operation GUNN, the purpose of which is to transport American personnel and radio equipment to Popesti Airdrome and establish positive and continuous point-to-point communications between this detachment and OSS (Office of Strategic Services, the forerunner of the Central Intelligence Agency) Bari. It is hoped that a successful execution of Operation GUNN will enable us to evacuate American air crew personnel from the Bucharest area to Italy.

"The first phase of Operation GUNN will be executed by three P-51 aircraft which will proceed to Bucharest area to verify friendly status of the airdrome. One of these P-51 aircraft, piloted by the Romanian officer, will land at Popesti Airdrome and signal the status of the airdrome to the other two aircraft by pyrotechnic flares. The other two aircraft will then relay this message in code by radio to Italy.

"The second phase of Operation GUNN will be to transport a detachment of communications personnel and their equipment to Popesti Airdrome. This phase of the operation will be carried out by two B-17s, escorted by thirty-two P-51s operating in two shifts of sixteen aircraft each."

The 15th's 306th Wing was ordered to provide the three P-51s and two pilots for the first phase and were told to land at Bari by 5 p.m. that very afternoon. By the next morning it was decided that four, rather than three, P-51s would be sent. The quartet, with Captain Cantacuzene at the controls of one, took off at 8 a.m. on August 29 for the flight to Bucharest, just thirteen hours after he and Gunn had landed at Bari. Each pilot was given a call sign. Cantacuzene's was Funnel; the other pilots would be referred to as Normal, Homemade and Cheerup. The Romanian didn't know it at the time but the American pilots flying back with him had been given secret orders to shoot him down if he behaved suspiciously on the way into Popesti. Operation Gunn was on.

At midmorning, the Romanian, now flying an American fighter, landed at Popesti while the other three pilots circled high above. The captain checked quickly. He had one of three signals to send aloft. A double yellow pyrotechnic flare would tell the other pilots that the airdrome was still firmly held by his countrymen and that it was clear for the B-17s to bring in the communications personnel. A double red flare would mean that it's unsafe for Allied aircraft to land. A single green would tell them to stand by for five more minutes. A fourth warning was also planned: if the three pilots aloft saw no flares within fifteen minutes of Cantacuzene's landing they were to assume that the airdrome was unsafe for the Allies and rush back to Bari.

The yellow flare came up and the three P-51s, as ordered, climbed high and sped westward to radio a U.S. weather plane which was circling halfway home over Yugoslavia. They passed on the safe condition report to the weather plane which relayed it to Bari.

Bigfence was the call sign of their radio contact back in Italy, and the message Bari received was this: "Hello Bigfence, this is Normal, I have six zero six gallons of gas, repeat six zero six." The coded message meant that Popesti was safe and the B-17s—gassed, crewed and ready to roll—could be dispatched.

If the message had been "Hello Bigfence, this is Normal, ceiling and visibility zero zero, repeat zero zero" then Bari would have known to keep the B-17s on the ground.

The 2nd Bomb Group of the 5th Wing had provided the two B-17s with full combat crews, full gas supply, full ammunition—but no bombs. They had arrived at Bari that morning before the P-51s left for Popesti Airdrome and were fitted with special bomb bay racks for loading personnel and equipment. Also on board were special agents from the OSS. By 10 a.m. they were ready, waiting only for Bigfence to get the radio message from Normal. Takeoff was scheduled for no more than thirty minutes after the affirmative message came in.

The big bombers lifted off from Bari at fifteen minutes past high noon, accompanied by their escort of thirty-two P-51s from the 31st Fighter Group of the 306th Wing for the three-hour flight to Bucharest. The mission's orders called for eight of the fighters to increase speed thirty miles from Popesti, leave the formation, circle the airdrome for an additional flare signal from the ground, and return to the formation. Their signal to the B-17s that it was okay to land at Popesti would be a series of small dives and zooms, a standard landing signal. If they rocked their wings— a danger signal—the bomber pilots were to turn for home.

With a positive signal at 3:30 p.m., the two B-17s circled the field to the left with wheels down and settled in atop the pockmarked, weed-covered runway at Popesti while the P-51s provided cover overhead. It was the first time Allied planes had landed in Romania without being forced down or shot out of the skies.

The 15th Air Force orders had told the bomber commanders: "After landing, the B-17s will be unloaded as rapidly as possible. If any American personnel are at the airdrome available for immediate loading, a maximum of ten per B-17 may be evacuated to Italy. B-17s must unload and take off again as quickly as possible since endurance of P-51s covering the airdrome will be very limited." It was a well-understood message: get in, unload fast, don't wait for passengers, and get out before the P-51s run out of fuel.

The landing party of twelve was led by Colonel George W. Kraiger, who for several months had been in charge of much smaller rescue missions in the Balkans. Others in the team were to handle communications. The dozen men got their equipment off the planes quickly and waved goodbye as the two B-17s — engines still running — turned and zoomed back down the runway. Their welcoming party was friendly and included Rica Georgesou, the Romanian secretary of state and minister of national economy, who accompanied the American team into Bucharest to meet with other Romanian officials. One of their first problems was in trying to arrange for enough trucks and buses to carry the prisoners from various camps to the Popesti Airdrome. They estimated that about eight hundred men were at the camp on the southwest side of Bucharest, the largest site. But a hundred were at another camp in a nearby town, plus those in the hospital and an uncertain number hiding within the city.

The next day, Colonel Kraiger went to the POW hospital to inform the patients of plans for their evacuation the following day. He counted fifty-one there, including thirty-nine bed patients and twelve ambulatory cases.

The landing party had brought in Red Cross kits for the hospital patients but little else. After all, it was a rescue mission, not an attempt to make living conditions better for the long haul. The team also made contact with the commander of Russian troops in the area and told him of the plan to start the evacuation the next day, August 31. The Russian agreed. But the American OSS agents ran into a snag. Between technical problems and atmospheric conditions they were unable to contact Bari by radio.

That afternoon, the team and senior officers among the POWS completed their plans for the evacuation to begin the next day. Attempts to reach Bari by radio were still unsuccessful, so Captain Cantacuzene was called upon again to fly back to Italy. He lifted off from Popesti in his American P-51 at 5:15 p.m. on August 30 armed with a letter from the team with the necessary information to begin the evacuation.

Earlier, a flight of B-17s had been sent to bomb airfields north of Bucharest. That put an end to the German bomber attacks on the prisoners, but the 15th Air Force commanders back in Bari knew that German fighter aircraft were still within range of the city and could interrupt and possibly destroy any attempt to get the prisoners out.

Meanwhile, Kraiger was organizing the movement of prisoners to Popesti Airdrome. He had found some eight hundred men in the main camp on the outskirts of Bucharest, where they had moved to avoid the heavy German bombing in the middle of the city. He also found another hundred in the nearby town of Pitrositza and dozens of others scattered throughout the area. Romanian officials came up with twenty-seven buses for Kraiger which they moved to the main camp by 5 a.m. on August 31. By 6 a.m. all eight hundred prisoners there had been moved to Popesti.

Kraiger then commandeered a truck and had men scouring the city for bread and cheese to feed those at the airdrome. Next, he lined the men up along the edge of the field in groups of twenty at 150-foot intervals and designated a leader for each group. Thus, when the B-17s arrived each could taxi up to a group, load and be ready to take off.

With plans completed to evacuate the prisoners, the stage was set for act two.

8 OPERATION REUNION

One of the problems faced by the POWs, the rescue team and Romanian officials was in contacting the scattered prisoners in and near Bucharest, those who had returned to the vicinity of the prison camps and those still hiding throughout the city. No general announcement could be made to reach them for fear of alerting German spies and pockets of German troops to the rescue effort. Instead, the news was spread from man to man, alone or in groups, throughout the city streets, in bombed-out buildings, at the hospital, at and around the camps—wherever they could be found. And it was done in whispers: "Tomorrow morning. Be at Popesti Airdrome. We're leaving."

Back in Bari, the 15th Air Force, armed with the letter carried by Captain Cantacuzene, was ready. They had prepared thirty-eight B-17s from the 2nd and 97th Bomb Groups of the 5th Wing as transports for Operation Reunion, the largest evacuation of its kind in history. Two-thirds of those bombers would fly two missions to Bucharest in the next two days. In addition, 94 P-38 fighters from the 1st, 14th and 82nd Fighter Groups and 158 P-51s from the 31st, 325th and 332nd Fighter Groups of the 306th Wing were quickly assembled to provide air cover for the B-17s. The preparations clicked like clockwork.

After all, this was more than a routine mission. This was all about rescuing and perhaps saving the lives of more than one thousand friends and comrades.

* * * * *

An interesting sidelight of the selection of escorts for the B-17s is lost in number designations for modern readers. One of the P-51 groups mentioned — the 332nd — is better known today as the Tuskegee Airmen, a group of pilots made famous by one factor: all were black men competing in a largely white world at a time when segregation of the races was still running rampant in the United States. The U.S. War Department had concluded that black men could not be combat pilots be-cause — the army let itself be told — blacks were inferior to whites. Under political pressure from Washington, led by none other than President Franklin Delano Roosevelt, the depart-ment and the Army Air Corps finally relented and allowed blacks to enter an experimental all-black unit at Chanute Army Air Field in Illinois in March 1941. Ground crews for the new unit, the 99th Pursuit Squadron, began training there. Four months later, pilot training began at Tuskegee Army Air Field in Alabama, next to the famous Tuskegee Institute. The first group of five black pilots graduated at Tuskegee as fighter pi-lots in March 1942. As time went on, almost a thousand more young, black Americans won their wings at Tuskegee.

Despite the achievement of becoming pilots as well as army officers, the black men still operated under segregated conditions in the country, even to the point of being denied access to white officer clubs at army bases. When other squad-rons joined the original 99th, the designation of the Tuskegee Airmen was changed to the 332nd Fighter Group, a unit of the 15th Air Force in Italy. But the color line still kept them on the sidelines as they flew obsolete P-39s on coastal patrol. Pres-sure from their officers — also blacks — finally forced the army to give the Tuskegee Airmen the more powerful P-47 Thun-derbolts and later the P-51, a fighter capable of escorting heavy bombers deep into German territory. Their fame as skilled pilots began to grow and so did their pride. They painted the tails of their planes red and soon became known to friend and foe alike as the Red Tails. Later, American bomber crews who gained life-saving protection on missions from the Tuskegee Airmen would refer to them as Red Tail Angels.

That reputation as skilled fighter pilots was no doubt a factor in assigning the 332nd to the important mission of rescuing so many prisoners from Romania. During the war, the Tuskegee Airmen never lost one of their escorted bombers to enemy fighters in some two hundred missions over German territory. They flew more than 15,000 sorties in the war — a sortie being one plane on one mission. They shot down 111 German fighters and destroyed 150 German aircraft on the ground. They destroyed 950 railcars, trucks and other German vehicles. They even sank a German ship. But sixty-six Tuskegee pilots were killed in action and thirty-three became prisoners of war.

Despite their outstanding record, the Tuskegee Airmen continued through the war as the 332nd Fighter Group, still a segregated unit. It wasn't until 1948, three years after the war, that President Harry S Truman ordered the end of segregation in America's armed forces.

* * * * *

The B-17s were told to fly at medium altitudes — about ten thousand feet — and below the cloud base, if possible. They would carry full fuel loads but, to minimize weight, a reduced load of ammunition. Their fighter escorts would remain aloft while the bombers landed, providing continuous air cover for the rescue. The fighters were told to track and destroy any enemy fighters appearing in the target area, but not to attack any other planes or strafe any ground targets. However, one group of P-51s was ordered to another target: a German air base near the town of Reghin 150 miles north-northwest of Bucharest, where they would strafe any aircraft on the ground.

Each wave of bombers was given a call sign, which included such names as Vealpie, Breakfast, Homemade and Reward, and their fighter escort groups had call signs such as Gasstove, Highgang, Sulphur and Squander.

On August 31, 1944, at 10 a.m., the first twelve Flying Fortresses lumbered into Popesti, protected overhead by an armada of fighters. Each B-17 carried a skeleton crew of six: pilot, copilot, navigator, engineer/top turret gunner, radio operator/gunner, and tail gunner. On one side of the abandoned field, the bomber crewmen could see hundreds of men sitting, or standing or lying as close to the runway as safety dictated. The pilots found the runway in bad shape, sometimes almost invisible due to weeds, pockmarked by shell and bomb holes, cluttered with chunks of concrete. Of the first twelve planes in, one blew a tire but came to a safe stop. On board another were two medical doctors — Lieutenant Colonel W. R. Lovelace and Major Raymond Beal — carrying badly needed medical supplies. The dozen B-17s were only on the ground for thirty minutes, long enough to stop, turn around, unload the doctors and their supplies and pull or push up to twenty-nine POWs into each of their cold, metal bellies. By 10:30, eleven of them were airborne again.

Lovelace and Beal were rushed to the POW hospital to prepare patients for the rescue. While Beal worked to make sure the wounded and sick were ready to move, Lovelace was out looking for trucks or buses to transport them. Beal found that the fifty-one men had received practically no medical care from Romanian medical officers during the three previous days due to the dangers from German bombers pounding Bucharest. It made his job more difficult in the face of the timetable to get most of these men out on the last flights of the day, now just hours away. He was able to prepare ten litter cases and twenty-nine ambulatory cases for those flights. And Lovelace, with help from POW officers and Romanian officials, got the needed transportation.

At 11:15 a.m., the second dozen B-17s landed, loaded and were up again by 11:45.

The third group of twelve bounced in at 12:15 and in twenty-five minutes all but one were off with their narrow fuselages crammed full of ex-prisoners. The twelfth plane in that group had sprung a serious oil leak and stayed on the ground.

At 1:15, two B-17s, specially fitted inside as ambulances with doctors among the crew, set down on the Popesti strip. The patients readied by Beal and Lovelace were loaded on board, strapped in and prepared for the ride to Bari. At 2:25 both planes took off, followed instantly by the B-17 which had been delayed with a now-repaired oil leak, and arrived at Bari at 5:45 p.m. All of the patients were immediately transferred to the military hospital there.

The first day of Operation Reunion had ended without a hitch. Neither the B-17s nor the men on the ground were attacked. Other than an oil leak and a flat tire—which kept one plane grounded overnight—there were no accidents or breakdowns. And with their fighter escorts the B-17s were safely back at Bari before the afternoon ended.

Thirty-eight B-17s had landed and thirty-seven had departed for Bari. They carried to freedom 739 airmen who had been incarcerated for up to thirteen months, including ten litter cases and twenty-nine ambulatory patients.

The next day, September 1, Operation Reunion Two got under way. Sixteen B-17s came in at 11:45 a.m. and, for a while, it looked like a possible disaster was developing. The left wing panel on one of the big bombers exploded upon landing. One hour later, fifteen of those planes were leaving, jammed through the mid-sections with evacuees. They were accompanied by a sixteenth plane, the B-17 which had blown a tire the previous day and had been repaired overnight.

The B-17s that day had salvaged 393 more lives, including the remainder of the patients and attendants from the POW

Prisoners at Popesti Airdrome in Romania are lined up as a B-17 in the background taxis up to load them aboard for the flight to freedom.

Courtesy of U.S. Air Force Historical Research Agency, Maxwell AFB

Rescuers with military ambulances assist former prisoners deplaning from a B-17 in Italy.

Courtesy of U.S. Air Force Historical Research Agency, Maxwell AFB

Shortly after their arrival at an American air base in Italy, released prisoners of war in a wide variety of clothing await delousing to rid themselves of vermin. Some of these men, as a slap at their captors, were wearing highly ranked Nazi medals that they had bought in Bucharest for ten cents each.

Courtesy of U.S. Air Force Historical Research Agency, Maxwell AFB

hospital. At Bari, forty-one men who had not been in the Bucharest hospital were immediately hospitalized for observation and treatment.

On September 2, while Colonel Kraiger was thanking the Romanian president, prime minister and other government leaders for their assistance, a few more POW stragglers came in. At the main prison camp, nineteen men were preparing for evacuation the following day when Russian troops began filling the camp with captured Germans. Throughout the city, Americans who had been taken in by wealthy Romanian families finally got the word that the last planes would be leaving the next day.

On September 3, Operation Reunion Three began with the landing of two B-17s and one C-47 troop transport at 11:30 a.m. The C-47 carried a repair crew, tools and—strapped under its fuselage—a wing panel for the B-17 which had been stranded two days earlier. At 1:15 p.m., a flight of thirteen P-51s designated as the return escort to Bari landed for refueling. And at 3:30, the C-47, all three B-17s and the P-51 escorts were in the air for the trip to Italy. They were carrying the repair crew, Colonel Kraiger, and the final twenty-nine POWs who were able to be evacuated.

Their mission had been accomplished. Those Allied airmen who returned to their bases after the 1942 and 1943 Ploesti attacks and the thousands who got back safely during the 1944 blitz of late spring and summer, those who had escaped capture and returned to friendly territory, those who died in the effort, and those POWs who had been rescued in a daring operation had together successfully cut off the main source of precious oil to German army, navy and air forces. When Russian troops moved into Ploesti on August 30, they reported the eleven mammoth refineries were ruined. There was no oil flowing and none would flow from there again in the German cause. The Ploesti airmen had suffered greatly but they had also pulled the plug on Hitler.

When Operation Reunion ended, only one man was left behind. Technical Sergeant Peter Tierney of the 460th Bomb Group was still hospitalized with double phlebitis of the legs and septicemia (blood poisoning) resulting from wounds. He was too ill to be moved immediately. Two American doctors, armed with medical supplies, were left there to care for him until an evacuation could be safely undertaken.

After the prisoners had been taken out, Romanian authorities published notices in their newspapers and broadcast messages that any stranded American or British fliers still in the country were to report to the Hotel Ambassador in Bucharest. Agents from the OSS remained in Bucharest to assist any such men. The 15th Air Force, in postwar reports, did not indicate whether any additional prisoners were found.

In his report, Kraiger wrote that the "Romanian Provisional Government and Romanian Air Force gave wholehearted cooperation in this evacuation."

Operation Reunion, planned and executed in a relatively short period of time, was a rousing success. No lives were lost; no one was injured; and only one American plane, a P-38, was lost. In three days, 1,127 Americans, 31 British, two Dutch naval officers (including an admiral) and one French sergeant were released from captivity and—in just a few hours—returned to safety, medical treatment, food, water and the guarantee that they would be going home. The Americans included 445 officers and 608 enlisted men from the 15th Air Force and 30 officers and 44 enlisted men from the 8th and 9th Air Forces. The British included twenty fliers from the RAF and two soldiers from the British army.

One of the B-17s also carried a stowaway, a twenty-nine-year-old man who claimed to have been born in Battle Creek, Michigan, of Romanian parents. While trying to get a seat on one of the rescue planes, he told American authorities that he and his parents had returned to Romania when his grandparents died in 1927. They were there, he said, to claim property left by the grandparents and told the government they were still Romanian citizens. The man informed Colonel Kraiger that he established his claim to American citizenship in 1941 and got a passport from the Romanians for passage to America but could not get a visa from the Germans. In the three intervening years, he said he was interned twice by the Germans. Two American pilots who were prisoners gave him GI coveralls and an identification card belonging to one of the pilots in an attempt to get him on one of the B-17s. Kraiger, doubting the man's story and fully aware that he as a U.S. officer was responsible for evacuating the Allied POWs, refused to let him board. But the man did manage to stow away on a later flight and was immediately taken into custody upon landing at Bari. The air force reports did not indicate what happened to him at that point.

The rescuers were not without opposition. Fighters which had bombed and strafed German airfields north of Bucharest ran into moderate flak around Ploesti. They encountered and shot down two German bombers and fought two German ME-109s, one of which was damaged.

Sergeant Fritz, though not hospitalized at Bucharest, was one of those so painfully ill that he had to be helped aboard a B-17 on the second day. He recalls that Popesti Airdrome, including the runway, looked more like a farm field than an airport. He figured it was less than three hundred feet from the tall cement building where he had sought refuge from the German bombing to the taxiway where the bombers—their four engines still whining—paused while crewmen pulled, pushed or carried the POWs into the planes.

Fritz was so anxious to leave that he found the strength to walk that distance and the patience to wait until his group was ushered out to a waiting plane. As he waited to board he was struck by how the B-17s seemed to be bouncing down the pitted runway, a runway so covered by weeds that he could not tell whether the planes were on it or off it.

As he waited he couldn't help but smile at this ragtag bunch: some in dirty, faded uniforms; some in bits of civilian clothing; some wearing enemy helmets and carrying souvenirs; some in possession of more bottles of wine than it appeared they could carry. Many were wearing pants which had come from a Red Cross shipment before the prison was abandoned. All of the pants were size forty, so these starving airmen couldn't fill them and used any means to hold them up.

When it was his turn to board he tried to hurry but could only manage a controlled walk to the hulking bomber. Someone pulled him in. He glanced around; there seemed to be about twenty prisoners inside. Whether it was planned or just forgotten in the rush, there were no parachutes on board for these men. That bothered Fritz. The last time he was in a plane it was going down, he had a parachute, and it saved his life.

As soon as everyone was aboard and the bomb bay doors were closed, the B-17 revved back to the runway. Fritz recalls the takeoff roll on that bumpy field was quite rough. He could feel the wheels banging into potholes and wondered if they would blow a tire. He had become accustomed to relatively smooth runways. He worried that they wouldn't get off the ground, but, finally, they did. For whatever reason— he doesn't know why—he stayed on his knees for the roll down the runway rather than lie down or sit with his back against the metal side. But when the loaded bomber finally nosed up and the wheels broke free of Mother Earth, his nerves settled a bit and he sat on the hard, cold metal floor.

Once aloft, the B-17s circled until all in the group were airborne. They formed up surrounded by the fighter escorts and headed west, across Romania and then Yugoslavia, over the Adriatic, headed for Italy. Except for the flights carrying the hospital patients, neither doctors nor medics were aboard to check on immediate problems. Extra bodies like that would have just taken up space needed for the freed prisoners. There was no food or anything to drink. All that would be available in quality and quantity within hours. The mission was to get everyone out, as safely and quickly as possible. Fritz, a half century later, remembers it as "a rough trip."

There was time for some men to talk, to compare notes. They generally agreed that they were treated badly by their captors, particularly the Germans. They had not been required to work, even though the rules of the Geneva Convention allowed work details for captured enlisted men. The food — what little they had — was not too bad. The Romanian guards had been friendly, unlike the Germans. But depression was still quite evident, obviously deeply set in the minds of these men. They were still aboard bombers which could be shot down or crash due to mechanical problems, so safety remained a concern. But they were also, at least inwardly, relieved that they were finally out of captivity. Many would learn that depression would remain with them, in some cases for the rest of their lives. It had been ground into their very souls by the waiting, the unknown future, the separation from home, the hunger, and the pain of injury or illness as prisoners of war.

Fritz and many others needed help to crawl from the B-17s after they landed at Bari hours later. The trip back had been tough on everyone, particularly the sick and wounded. The big bombers were not built for comfort. The ex-prisoners could only lie or kneel or sit on the bare steel, still hungry and still in need of medical attention but at last away from the camp and Bucharest and heading home, at least to a military home.

As each B-17 landed at Bari during the three-day operation, it was met by one of the 15th Air Force generals. At one such greeting, the unit's commanding officer, General Nathan Twining, shouted: "Thank God, you're back. We've sweated you out a long time." The men were told they'd soon be going home and then ambulances took the litter cases to the hospital.

Before they got into a building or too close to many people at Bari the other ex-POWs were taken to a yard off the runway and told to strip off all clothing, which was then burned. Each man was sprayed with powder to kill lice all over, particularly where body hair was heavy such as heads and armpits and the genital area, even up the rectum. Then they were given clean and temporary clothing. "Nothing fit," recalls Fritz, "but nothing had to."

They were trucked to the hospital for a quick check of heart, lungs and feet; those with problems were kept for treatment. Those who desired could request a full medical examination. Next came sandwiches and hot coffee, the filling out of government forms and assignment to quarters.

Later, they would be brought clothing from their own footlockers. Then came the questions, a formal interrogation from intelligence personnel about life in a prisoner-of-war camp.

Back at Foggia, Fritz discovered that someone had stolen a two-dollar pipe from his footlocker. It never prevented him from smoking a pipe though, a habit he continued into the twenty-first century.

A report filed by Lieutenant Colonel R. B. Nelson of the Medical Corps said this:

"All the patients interviewed observed that the general standard of the medical care which they received in Romania was much lower than that to which they have become accustomed

Freed American prisoners and their clothing are sprayed to kill lice after their arrival in Italy.

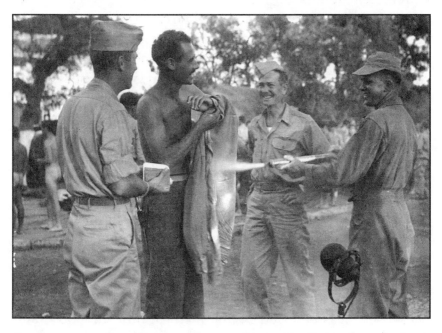

One ex-prisoner talks with Army Air Force officers as his clothing is sprayed with a delousing agent.

in the United States. They noticed that the doctors, in general, did not appear to be well trained although there were, of course, some exceptions to this observation. The nursing care was poor and there was a great scarcity of all types of medical supplies and equipment. Sulfa drugs were unobtainable and the supplies of morphine were limited. On the other hand, those patients who received medical attention from the Germans before being released to the Romanians observed that their equipment was good and their medical supplies ample. This caused some bitterness on the part of the Romanian medical officers, who complained that while the Germans had ample medical supplies, they would not release these materials to the Romanians.

"The low general standard of medical proficiency reported by our airmen is confirmed by a review of the hospitalized cases. The statements of the patients, that amputations of the extremities were performed by the slightest provocation, are supported by the large number of such cases among our evacuees. This is partly explained by the fear of infection, on the part of the Romanian doctors, a fear somewhat justified because of the lack of drugs. This, however, would not explain some of the amputations which appeared to result from their policy 'when in doubt, amputate'. Examination of x-ray films brought back by Lt. Col. Lovelace tends to confirm the impression that the orthopedic work, in general, was not of a high standard.

"During the time many of the evacuees were prisoners of war, an outbreak of diphtheria occurred in the area in which they were located. The treatment used in the high number of cases of neuritis following these attacks is of interest. The large number of injections which the patients received leads one to believe that a preparation of very low potency must have been used. It is believed by the medical officers who examined these cases in the (American) Hospital that as high as ninety percent of the cases of diphtheria were followed by a typical post diphtheritic neuritic syndrome. The explanation of this high percentage of complications is not clear. Deficient diet would appear to be factor but one (man) who contracted the disease one week after his capture also developed this complication. The time element in this case would not appear to be sufficient to account for the neuritis on the basis of dietary deficiency."

Dr. Nelson's report also touched briefly on prison hospital food and treatment. He wrote:

"In general, the food in the hospitals was poor, consisting much of the time in soup and black bread. Vegetables were occasionally obtained but meat was rarely served. Sanitary conditions were also far from satisfactory.

"Interviews with the evacuated patients did not reveal any evidence of organized discrimination against the Americans. Conditions were generally bad but, in most instances, our fliers reported that the situation was as unsatisfactory for the Romanian patients as for the Americans. The limited supply of drugs, in most instances, was used for the cases which needed treatment most, regardless of nationality."

The Army Air Force did not try to blot out the Romanian experience in a flood of secret documents. Indeed, they took steps to make sure the world knew about it. Seven war correspondents were allowed to fly into Popesti aboard the B-17s to get first-hand stories about Operation Reunion while other reporters flocked to Bari in special military flights. The army's 1st Combat Camera Unit shot newsreel film with sound and still photos in Bucharest. Four of those still shots were radioed immediately to the United States and some forty additional pictures were sent via plane to Washington for distribution.

Six of the freed airmen were flown to Rome for interviews by war correspondents and live radio broadcasts which were beamed back to the States. A military radio program—the Army Hour—even revised its schedule at the last minute so that it could include interviews with Colonel Gunn and the interned officer who assisted him in launching the rescue, a Major Yeager.

Lieutenant I. H. Fox, one of the prisoners, wrote a series of six articles describing life in the Bucharest camps and the entry of Russian troops into the city, copies of which were given to the correspondents in Rome.

It was estimated that some 150,000 words on Operation Reunion were filed by reporters for the wire services and newspapers back home. At the time, it was regarded by war correspondents in Italy as the biggest air story up to that time.

Between August 1, 1943, the day of the "low-level" Ploesti raid, and August 23, 1944, when the Romanian government switched sides, an estimated 2,500 American and British airmen were reported missing in action over Romania. Most of them—2,290—were lost during the 15th Air Force's extensive and ongoing attacks against the oil refineries from April 5 to August 20, 1944. By August 23, 867 of those men who had escaped or successfully resisted capture had found their way back to Italy, mainly through Yugoslavia. Of the remaining 1,400, more than three-fourths were spirited out of Romania in Operation Reunion, which the 15th Air Force claimed was "without precedent for size, speed or success." Indeed, 15th officers predicted it would become "a model for further rescue operations as other Nazi areas succumb to the Allied offensive."

9 ◇ GOING HOME

On September 4, 1944, Harry Fritz was handed an official letter from the 15th Air Force. Here's what it said:

"Dear Sergeant Fritz, You are going home. With you will go the thanks and admiration of the 15th Air Force for a superb and heroic performance. You are the returning heroes of the Battle of Ploesti. You will be greeted and treated as such by your loved ones, and by a grateful American public. They are proud of you.

"Your safe return to my command marked the culmination of an outstanding campaign in the annals of American military history. The German war machine's disintegration on all fronts is being caused, to a large extent, by their lack of oil—oil that you took from them.

"I have only one regret on this jubilant occasion. I wish it had been possible to bring out of Romania every officer and man who went down in that battle. Unfortunately, there are some who will never return. The memory of their sacrifice is an inspiration to all of us.

"One of the memories of my life will be the thrill I experienced as the B-17s came into view, circled, landed and I saw you unloading. It was impossible for me to greet each of you and it will be impossible for me to say 'goodbye' to each of you before you return to the States. However, I do want you to know my thoughts and those of your fellow soldiers are with you.

"Best of luck and Godspeed."

The letter was signed by Major General Nathan F. Twining, the 15th's commander.

Later, Fritz learned that his parents were not notified that he was free until September 18, two weeks after the rescue. A telegram from Washington said simply: "Am pleased to inform you your son, Staff Sergeant Harry B. Fritz, returned to military control." Three days later they received another telegram from Washington. It said: "Supplementing my recent message, am pleased to inform you your son, Staff Sergeant Harry B. Fritz, has been returned to military control and is enroute to United States by ship and expected to arrive about 28 September. He will be given opportunity to communicate with you upon arrival and granted furlough at an early date."

At a ceremony in Italy on September 8, Fritz was one of eighteen men awarded the Soldier's Medal for helping wounded prisoners in the Bucharest hospital before Operation Reunion brought them all back to Italy. At the time, his body was still weak and his mind was still foggy and he couldn't remember exactly what he did at the hospital to help others. "I didn't think I had helped anyone," he says. But the army said he had and that it was during the three days of German air raids over his camp.

A citation accompanying the medal read: "For heroism at great risk of life during the period from August 24 to August 26. Volunteering to evacuate wounded American flyers who had been interned in an enemy prison hospital in Romania, these gallant men, during an intense and heavy bombardment and strafing attack lasting continuously for over 48 hours, carried wounded personnel to air-raid shelters and also carried medical supplies, bedding, food and clothing from blasted and burning buildings in order to insure the comfort and safety of

The filing time shown in the date line on telegrams and day letters is STANDARD TIME at point of origin. Time of receipt is STANDARD TIME at point of destination

1 HG   16 Govt   WUX   Washington DC   6.27 PM 9-18-44

Mrs Lillian I.Fritz
249 South Main St
Pine Grove,Penn.

            Am pleased to inform you your son Staff Sergeant

Harry B.Fritz returned to military control.

            J.A.ULIO The Adjutant General.
                        825 AM 19th

Second telegram tells Fritz's parents that he has been rescued, but is dated more than two weeks after he arrived back in Italy.

Harry Fritz Collection

The filing time shown in the date line on telegrams and day letters is STANDARD TIME at point of origin. Time of receipt is STANDARD TIME at point of destination

2 HG   64 Gov't   7 Extra dupe foned fm 20" confirm in AM .

                 WUX Washington DC. 8.44 PM 9-21-44

Mrs.Lillian I.Fritz
249 South Main St
Pine Grove,Pa.
            Supplementing my recent message am pleased to inform
you your son Staff Sergeant Harry B.Fritz has been returned to Military
control and is enroute to United States by ship and expected to arrive
about twenty eight September period He will be given opportunity to
communicate with you upon arrival and granted furlough at an early date

                 ULIO The Adjutant General.
                        8.30AM 22nd.

Third telegram gives Fritz's parents details on when he should return home.

Harry Fritz Collection

*FALVO LOUIS	2	LT	0-687824	RMI	RUM 484
*FARIS JAMES E JR	2	LT	0-695361	RCA	RUM 449
*FASOLAS CHARLES E	S	SC	33286674	RCA	RUM 450
FENYES JAMES J	T	SG	33390830	RMI	RUM 97
*FEORE JOSEPH V	2	LT	0-818567	RMI	YUG 459
*FERGUSON TRUMAN E	SGT		18232791	RMI	YUG 459
FERGUSON GEORGE W	S	SC	32267533	RCA	RUM 301
FERNANDEZ RENEE	S	SC	39555339	RCA	RUM 449
*FERRELL OTIS B	2	LT	0-818564	RMI	YUG 459
*FIDLER JACKSON H	SGT		38370393	RMI	RUM 301
FILI WILLIAM J	S	SG	13151977	RCA	RUM 450
*FILKORN HARRY	2	LT	0-699050	RCA	RUM 464
FINGER LOUIS J	2	LT	0-706723	RMI	RUM 459
*FINKELSTEIN MAX H	CPL		19203089	RCA	RUM 1
*FINLEY MORRIS E	2	LT	0-669261	RCA	RUM 465
*FISHER SIDNEY	S/FLO		7-061539	RCA	RUM 465
*FISHER THEODORE R	S	SC	35576200	RMI	RUM 454
*FISHER DAVID W	2	LT	0-701585	RMI	ITA 459
*FISH IRVING D JR	1	LT	0-706724	RMI	RUM 98
*FITZ ELWOOD A	2	LT	0-817648	RMI	RUM 450
*FLAHERTY EDWARD F JS	SG		12185275	RCA	RUM 99
*FODEN KENNETH C	SGT		32863848	RCA	RUM 465
*FOGEL ANTHONY	2	LT	0-686688	RCA	RUM 455
FOGLE LINWOOD L	T	SC	14169508	RMI	RUM 98
*FOLEY WILLIAM J JR	S	SC	31325451	RMI	RUM 301
*FONTANA RICHARD C	J2	LT	0-751994	RCA	RUM 463
*FONTENEAU RICHARD	A2	LT	0-807406	RCA	RUM 463
*FOOR HERBERT L	2	LT	0-826129	RMI	RUM 1
*FORSHAGE FELIX C	2	LT	0-690644	RCA	RUM 449
*FOSTER JOHN C	S	SC	39121479	RCA	RUM 450
*FOSTER DANIEL E	T	SC	35283693	RMI	RUM 376
*FOSTER ALSON B	T	SC	20454253	RMI	RUM 376
*FOWLER GEORGE E	SGT		39532393	RCA	RUM 459
*FOX IRVING H	1	LT	0-674749	RMI	RUM 99
FOX CHARLES S	CPL		31307668	RMI	RUM 454
*FRANK EDWARD W	T	SG	12049702	RCA	RUM 376
*FRANKS JAMES R	2	LT	0-694443	RCA	RUM 449
FRANTZ ARTHUR S	2	LT	0-701246	RMI	RUM 454
*FRANCO JOHN F	S	SC	15070191	RCA	RUM 455
*FREESTONE EARL C	2	LT	0-763150	RMI	RUM 98
*FRITZ HARRY B	S	SC	33686413	RMI	RUM 376
FUGERE LUCIEN C	T	SC	11008547	RCA	RUM 449
*FULTON HAROLD D	S	SC	37581338	RMI	RUM 99
*FUNK GLENFERD E	1	LT	0-735563	RCA	RUM 465
*GAGHAN JOHN E	S	SC	12093100	RMI	RUM 99
*GALATI JOHN S	2	LT	0-688954	RCA	RUM 449
*GALLANT ALFRED J	S	SC	31151569	RCA	RUM 449
*GALL JAMES W	2	LT	0-748065	RMI	RUM 455
*GALVIN JOHN J	S	SC	32761046	RMI	RUM 455
*GAMACHE HAROLD J	T	SC	16143427	RCA	RUM 450
*GAYNOR HARRY J	S	SC	12136576	RCA	RUM 455

Prisoner-of-war list carries the name of Staff Sergeant Harry Fritz (eleventh from bottom) and a few of the other 1,100 Allied airmen snatched from German hands in 1944.

Courtesy of U.S. Air Force Historical Research Agency, Maxwell AFB

the patients. Regardless of incessant sniping, strafing and bombing, these men, with complete disregard for their own safety, were instrumental in saving the lives of countless American and Allied wounded personnel. By their superb courage, valor and devotion to duty, these men have upheld the highest traditions of the Military Service, thereby reflecting great credit upon themselves and the Armed Forces of the United States of America."

On September 10, the ex-POWs were taken by special train to Naples to await the "first available water transportation" to the United States. They were billeted at the 19th Replacement Battalion where troops just coming to Europe to fight the war were being housed. Trucks would take the airmen directly from the barracks to the docks when their ships were ready. Meanwhile, comfort was the order of the day. Extra rations had been drawn so that all personnel had fresh meat and vegetables and additional supplies of candy and cigarettes. From the Red Cross came kits containing toilet articles, and more cigarettes. The men who were in the 8th and 9th Air Forces would be flown back to their units in Great Britain before sailing for home.

The civilian ships carrying wounded Americans and former POWs back home at times also contained civilians escaping the horrors of Europe. For example, one ship carried three members of a family named Katz — apparently sisters ranging in age from 14 to 21 — who were going to Brooklyn. All had been born in Hungary in the 1920s. The report indicated that their father — who was naturalized as an American in 1941 or 1942 — was waiting for them in New York. Not with them were their mother and a younger sister, who were among an estimated two to four million Jews gassed and cremated by the Nazis in the concentration camp at Auschwitz. For the Katz family and thousands of American servicemen, the war was over.

Still suffering from the effects of dysentery, Fritz, along with other ex-prisoners, left Naples on an old ship flying the

French flag. He never asked and never learned why a French ship was used, but it got him back to the States in thirteen days. "I think everybody got seasick, except me," he said. "It could have been that I was already too sick to worry about my first ocean voyage."

In New York City, the men from the Bucharest camp were taken to Fort Slocum for further processing. Once there he had to call home and ask his mother to send him a bit of spending money because during his time overseas he had sent home virtually his entire pay each month, a full ninety dollars. From Fort Slocum, the now-free POWs were shipped to Atlantic City for two weeks of rest and recreation at one of the big board-walk hotels which had been taken over by the army.

On a furlough home, he was invited to attend a public meeting held in the Necho Allen Hotel in nearby Pottsville. Mrs. Edward Finkenstaedt, a member of the national staff of the American Red Cross Prisoners of War Service, addressed some five hundred area residents that Sunday afternoon. She told them how to communicate with their relatives and friends who were still held in prison camps via letters and telegrams. Write often, she advised, but don't expect to receive too many letters because most prisoners are limited in the amount of mail they can send. Books must be sent directly from the pub-lisher, she said, but the Red Cross can send food packages and a "capture parcel" which contained thirty items of clothing and personal items.

Sergeant Fritz—his thin frame barely filling out his uni-form—was asked to address the large crowd. First, he told them that a prisoner is more concerned about his loved ones than himself.

"Write your boy and tell him you can take it, that you are well and not worried about him, that you know he will come through," he told the audience. Such a message, he continued, "is like food and he begins at once to have a new zest on life."

To assure those in the room of the treatment their loved ones were probably receiving in the camps, Fritz talked of his own experiences: "I was not treated too badly. While it is true that I lived on soup and bread for a short time in the prison camp it was not long before I received the Red Cross food package which changed my monotonous and untasty diet."

Fritz's tour of duty was not over. After recuperating from the weakness brought on by dysentery, he was assigned to the Primary Airplane and Engine Mechanics' school at Amarillo Army Airfield in Texas from February 6 to May 9, 1945. His next, and last, duty station was Lockport, Ohio, where he repaired B-17 engines.

On November 3, 1945, almost six months after the Germans had surrendered and less than three months following the surrender of Japan, Staff Sergeant Harry B. Fritz was discharged from the U.S. Army Air Corps.

Former Staff Sergeant Harry Fritz in the twenty-first century.

Harry Fritz Collection

Mr. and Mrs. Harry Fritz of Camp Hill, Pennsylvania.

Harry Fritz Collection

EPILOGUE

Harry Fritz's transition to civilian life in little Pine Grove, Pennsylvania, was difficult. He felt that his family and friends and neighbors expected him (and other combat veterans) to resume a normal civilian life. But it wasn't that easy. He had flashbacks of his experiences in the air, in a parachute and in a prison camp. He felt out of place and was concerned about the future. There was a great need to find some way of putting the war behind him. And he did, or so he thought.

"For six months I was a drunk," he freely admits. "No job to go to and just drink beer all day with my friends. Finally, my mother told me to sober up and get on with my life. And I did!"

Alcoholism was not an unusual step for men returning from captivity and the deep impressions that incarceration left in their minds.

More than a half century after his life-altering experiences in the skies above Europe and in a German prison camp, Fritz still attends monthly support meetings to discuss the nightmares he and other former POWs still have. For most of those fifty years he was extremely reluctant to discuss both his experiences and his emotions with anyone other than former POWs.

When asked how the men who fought World War II were able to cope with the demands of that conflict, Fritz attributes at least a part of it to the deprivations they faced growing up during the Great Depression.

He says that people who have never lost their freedom don't really know what freedom is. To this day, he still takes a daily and solitary walk around the block of comfortable small-town homes where he lives "just to feel free."

And he's still amazed at how the military accomplished its goals in the craziness of war, yet in peacetime continually needs to correct the record. Case in point: in the 1950s he received a call from the California Governor's Office asking if he could identify a man who claimed to have been shot down in Romania and imprisoned near Bucharest. The man had suggested that the Office write to Fritz after the army said he had never been in the camp. Fritz filled out a form sent from the Office, telling the governor that he certainly could identify him; it was a POW who had helped take care of Fritz when he was so sick.

At a POW/MIA program in 1995, Fritz listened intently as an army colonel talked about prisoners of war in general. He told his audience that prisoners had not given up the fight, but rather had no choice but to surrender. Some were prepared to give their lives for their country but none were prepared to be prisoners. Some, like Fritz, to this day have nightmares of torture, ill treatment or despair, perhaps of all three.

The speaker noted that medical problems among war prisoners grow the longer they're shut in. And, in a sense, some are always prisoners because they cannot forget the experience. They often develop mental health problems, going through depression, anger, guilt and sometimes suicidal tendencies. Some former prisoners, the colonel explained, think they are looked upon as having given up and are therefore the opposite of so-called heroes. Thus, they do not want to discuss their experience with anyone except other former POWs.

But, he continued, they did face harsh conditions, including the lack of food, housing and clothing; the absence of reasonable safety; the fear of beatings or other torture; frostbite, heat exhaustion and forced long and exhausting marches.

All need readjustment assistance with nutritional, psychological and often alcohol problems. They need spiritual aid and understanding and the support of fellow prisoners.

During World War II, some 130,000 American soldiers, airmen and sailors were prisoners of the enemy, including about 95,000 in German hands. A fourth of the total American prisoners were airmen. But those captured by the Germans had a better survival rate than those taken by the Japanese. Many did not survive. Many faced major problems once back in civilian life. Many can never forget the tragedy of their youthful years. The death rate of Americans in captivity in Europe has been estimated at 4 percent, far below that of Russian prisoners held by the Germans. Some three million Russians are believed to have died in Nazi hands. But the death rate of Americans held in Japanese camps was ten times greater than the German camps.[1]

Both Germany and the United States had signed the Geneva Convention accord regarding the treatment of war prisoners. But Hitler's SS troops and the Gestapo political wing had high disregard for the rules and violated them at will.

The normal behavior for a prisoner was to center his attention on his immediate surroundings, endeavoring to survive in an alien world. For some, the aim was to plan and execute escapes, though few were really successful and all were extremely dangerous, if not deadly. Many looked to their spiritual lives of the past or found new religious support to counter the effects of POW camps, using prayer to bolster their belief in future freedom or to sustain themselves when they faced the feeling of being forgotten. Most said that friendships with other prisoners were the ablest means of maintaining their sanity.

In addition to the hazards associated with escape attempts, many prisoners were weakened by the lack of food or a poor prison diet or disease to the point that escape was not an option. In most cases, prison camps were at least hundreds of miles from Allied lines. Men who could not speak the local languages faced a major disadvantage if escape was tried. Then there were the matters of proper identification papers, civilian clothing, money and a host of other problems.

Of the American prisoners in the European Theater in World War II, only between 1 and 2 percent actually tried to escape.[2]

Ex-prisoners like Fritz found that family and friends could not fully comprehend what it meant to be shot out of the sky, be captured and imprisoned. For some men, those civilians closest to them were at times disinterested or unsympathetic because they could not understand how their men could have been changed so much in the few years they were away. That type of reception kept men from discussing their feelings, although "talking about it" was often the best therapy for recovery. Instead, they sought out other ex-prisoners for consolation and understanding.[3]

No one knew for sure what the long-term effects would be of this condition, which came to be known after the Vietnam War as post-traumatic stress disorder. The symptoms were chronic nightmares, frightening flashbacks, debilitating depression and antisocial behavior. "Recent studies now indicate that approximately twenty-five percent of World War II combat veterans suffered unmistakable symptoms of traumatic stress, but among POWs the percentage was close to ninety."[4]

NOTES

USAMHI = U.S. Army Military History Institute, Carlisle Barracks, Carlisle, PA.
BIH = Ballantine's Illustrated History of the Violent Century.

INTRODUCTION

1. Maj. James F. Sunderman, *World War II in the Air – Europe* (New York, 1963), USAMHI.
2. Lt. Gen. Ira C. Eaker, *Air Power in the Mediterranean, November 1942–February 1945*, USAMHI.
3. Sunderman, *World War II in the Air – Europe*, USAMHI.
4. Barrie Pitt, editor-in-chief, *Ploesti: Oil Strike, BIH* (New York, 1974).
5. Ibid., p. 124.
6. Ibid., p. 129.
7. James Dugan and Carroll Stewart, *Ploesti: The Great Ground-Air Battle of 1 August 1943*, Random House (New York, 1962).

EPILOGUE

1. Lewis H. Carlson, *We Were Each Other's Prisoners* (HarperCollins Publishers Inc., 1997), introduction 17-19.
2. Ibid., 129.
3. Ibid., 230.
4. Ibid., 235.

SOURCES

Most of the detailed information on Operation Gunn and Operation Reunion came from 1,850 pages of declassified reports, records and letters released by the Mediterranean Allied Air Forces. That material is stored on microfilm and listed as IRIS 243457 in the files of the Air Force Historical Research Agency at Maxwell Air Force Base, Alabama.

General information on the war in Europe and particularly on air operations can be found in publications available at the U.S. Army Military History Institute at Carlisle Barracks, Carlisle, Pennsylvania. (Note: During World War II, the United States Air Forces were a unit of the Army.) Those publications include:

"Air Power in the Mediterranean, November 1942–February 1945," a brief review compiled by the Mediterranean Allied Air Forces under the command of Lieutenant General Ira C. Eaker, U.S. Army.

The Army Air Forces in World War II – Volume 3, edited by Wesley Craven and James Cate, published by The University of Chicago.

World War II in the Air – Europe edited by Major James F. Sunderman, U.S. Air Force, published by Bramhall House, New York.

For general reading on the subjects of World War II air battles, flying B-24 Liberators, the Ploesti raids and prisoner-of-war conditions, I recommend the following books:

Clash of Wings — World War II in the Air by Walter J. Boyne, published by Touchstone, New York.

50 Mission Crush by Lt. Col. Donald R. Currier, USAF (Ret.), published by Burd Street Press, Shippensburg, Pennsylvania.

Ploesti: The Great Ground-Air Battle of 1 August 1943 by James Dugan and Carroll Stewart, published by Random House, New York.

"Ploesti: Oil Strike" edited by Barrie Pitt and David Mason, from *Ballantine's Illustrated History of the Violent Century*, published by Ballantine Books, New York.

We Were Each Other's Prisoners: An Oral History of World War II American and German Prisoners of War by Lewis H. Carlson, published by HarperCollins, New York.

The Wild Blue by Stephen E. Ambrose, published by Simon and Schuster, New York.

ACKNOWLEDGMENTS

It's usually difficult to decide who should be thanked first of those who helped develop an idea into a readable book. In this project, it was not difficult. It took Harry Fritz an extended period of time to give approval for this book to be written because it is still difficult for him to recall the horrors he and many others lived through in wartime. But he agreed that it's important for veterans to tell their stories, if not to a public audience then at least to their families and friends. So my thanks and continuing friendship go out to Mr. Fritz for devoting his time and energies to interviews over several months so that this story might be told.

Many others contributed advice and assistance in seeking out sources, finding pertinent details, and suggesting other avenues of research. My mission began with a group of people who oversee a mammoth body of material that's known worldwide in the U.S. Army Military History Institute at Carlisle Barracks, Carlisle, Pennsylvania. The professional help given by Dr. Richard J. Sommers and library technician Richard Baker at Carlisle was invaluable.

The comparative air force agency was able to assist in homing in on a most important aspect of this work, the dramatic and daring rescue mission which freed more than 1,100

Allied airmen from internment in Romania. The Air Force Historical Research Agency at Maxwell Air Force Base in Alabama provided microfilm copies of more than 1,800 pages of declassified World War II reports, records and letters dealing directly with American fliers shot down and captured following raids on the gigantic Ploesti oil refineries and with their rescue in 1944. The willing and able staff there also provided photographs which added a second dimension to this story. My thanks go out to the people at Maxwell, particularly Mrs. Lynn Gamma, Dick Gamma, Ed Martinez, Essie Roberts and Dennis Case.

A wide range of photographic possibilities was also offered by the staff at the Smithsonian Air and Space Museum in Washington, D.C., and I thank Joe Pruden and Ralph Stell Jr. Valuable World War II pictures were also available from the National Archives and Records Administration in College Park, Maryland, and I appreciate the assistance from Donald L. Singer in that agency. In addition, I thank Dr. Jeffrey S. Underwood of the U.S. Air Force Museum at Wright-Patterson Air Force Base in Ohio for his guidance in locating photographs.

I thank two longtime friends for their encouraging words and advice in this project, and particularly for their willingness to share from their own experiences in the section I've entitled "Words from Veterans." Retired Air Force Lieutenant Colonel Donald R. Currier of Smithburg, Maryland, was a B-24 navigator with the 15th Air Force in Italy. Will Ketner of Harrisburg, Pennsylvania, was a B-17 pilot with the 8th Air Force in England.

Last, but not least, I thank my son, Jon Williams, an Air Force veteran, for taking time from his busy schedule as an airport fire chief to prepare the maps which appear in this book.

—William G. Williams

INDEX

126